Sargon Donabed

REMNANTS
OF HEROES

The Assyrian Experience

The continuity of the Assyrian heritage from Kharput to New England

ܬܘܒ ܟܬܒܐ ܕܪܝܫܝ ܐܝܣܪܐ ܕܒܣܝܪܐ ܘܒܩܪܝܬܐ
ܕܒܝܬ ܐܠܗܐ ܘܩܪܝܬܐ ܦܪܡܝ ܠܒܢ

Assyrian Academic Society Press
CHICAGO

Remnants Of Heroes

Library of Congress Cataloging-in-Publication Data:
Remnants of Heroes: The Assyrian Experience: The continuity of the Assyrian heritage from Kharput to New England
Donabed, Sargon

p.cm.
Includes Index

Contents: Assyrians Past and Present ---Town Life--- Dispersion --- Establishment in the US --- Famous Kharput Assyrians --- The Recent Years
DS59.A75 .D66 2003
Assyrians --- History
Assyrians --- Biography
Assyrians --- United States

Dewey class no.: 909/ . 04921 22

ISBN 0-9744450-7-X

Assyrian Academic Society Press: September 2003
Published in the US by AB Press

Thanks to all those who made the book possible: Fred Alkakos, Fred Aprim, Natalie Babella, Tom Clarke, Robert Karoukian, John Lanci, Erika Schluntz, and especially Firas Jatou.

Figure 1. Author in Kharput (June 2003)

For the Assyrians of Kharput

Nothing is greater than the mistake that many scholars make in assuming they understand the people they write about, or their experiences.

Contents

Figures

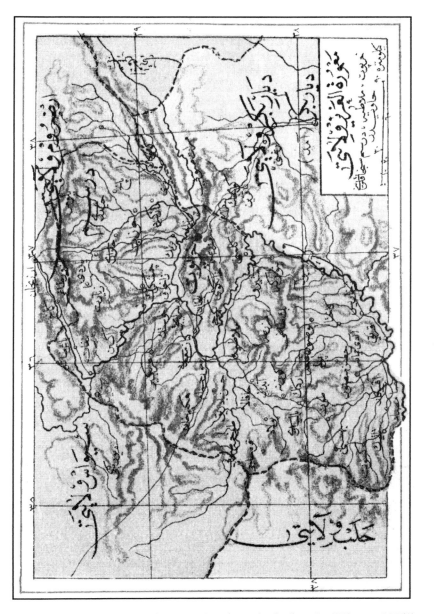

Figure 3. Map of the Eastern Ottoman Provinces including the "Kharput" Willayet

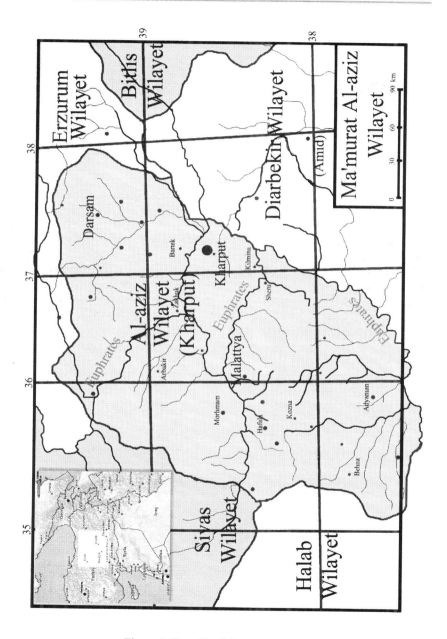

Figure 4. Cont. English translation.

Forward

As I was cleaning out the remains of my great aunt's old basement, I came across an old suitcase: musty and shabby from years of neglect. The straps on the outside showed signs of deterioration from age, bacteria, or whichever critter happened to find its aged fibers edible. I bent to examine the lock mechanism, and jumped when the slightest touch sent it springing open. As Pandora peered into her box, so did I gaze in amazement at my newly found treasure consisting of a bound collection of newspapers. The script was West Assyrian/Aramaic, and it was dated to the early part of the 20th Century in Beirut, Syria[1] entitled *Lichono d Omto*, "The Language of Nation ". I stared at my newfound fortune as a child upon a new bicycle. I could not help but think of the wisdom and untapped knowledge this rare find could offer.

Yet, I felt a sense of despair and depression at the thought that there are finds like this all over the world, lurking in basements. Who will be there to save them?

As I closed the suitcase, I stopped to ponder the future of the Assyrian people. What will become of our history, pictures, and personal experiences, and the memories and experiences of the past generations? Preservation is the key to immortality, or as close to it as we are likely to get. We must preserve our heritage for the future generations to learn our culture, and remember our struggles. This book is but an attempt at preserving the trials and tribulations of the Kharput[2] Assyrians.

---

[1] Modern Lebanon

[2] Kharput is also seen in its various spellings as Harput, Kharpert, Harpoot, and Kharpoot throughout this book.

Overview

This book charts the life, dispersion, and arrival to New England, of a small but extremely important segment of the Assyrian people; the Assyrians of the town of Kharput[2], in modern-day Turkey. How these people escaped the Assyrian Genocide of WWI, integrated into American society, and yet managed to retain their identity is central to understanding the perseverance of these people. By using first-hand oral accounts and stories, in addition to primary source documents, the goal is to give the reader a deep and personal view of these descendants of an ancient people, and their lives for the past 150 years.

In order to understand the Assyrians of Kharput, one must have knowledge of the Assyrian people in general. They are the descendents of the people of ancient Mesopotamia (Beth Nahrain), and its indigenous inhabitants. One of their wondrous city-states, Edessa, was the first kingdom to accept Christianity. Today, there are four main Christian Assyrian sects: Chaldean Uniate, Syriac Orthodox Church of Antioch, Syriac Catholic, and the Assyrian Church of the East. Some Maronites of Lebanon and the Yezidis[3] profess to being of the same stock as these modern Assyrians. In the Middle East, due to anti-indigenous sentiment of present regimes, the Assyrians are commonly referred to by these ecclesiastical designations.

Through the years, the Assyrians have been erroneously called Chaldeans, Suryani, Syriac, and various other names by their Near Eastern neighbors and Westerners; all these appellations are part of their heritage but fall short of its totality. The modern Assyrians are in fact the direct descendents of the ancient Assyrians. Indeed some self-proclaimed Syriac and Biblical "scholars" have made careers out of creating new names for the Assyrians. These pseudo-scholars have overlooked and ignored the truth in order to promote their outdated and inaccurate claims. The moot discussion that the terms *suraya* and *suroyo* are anything but variants of the word *Ashuraya/Ashuroyo* is bizarre.

---

[3] Attested to in an excerpt from Cheaney's *Expedition to the Euphrates and Tigris*. Harpers New Monthly Magazine volume 1 (Harper & Brothers: NY 1850 June to Nov.), 454.

Today, classical Assyrian (Syriac, Literary Syriac, *Līšānā Săprăyă*) is used primarily in the apostolic churches and by some writers. Most Assyrians use one of the modern dialects of the language. Syriac is a further development of ancient Assyrian-Aramaic, and remains heavily influenced by ancient Akkadian. Assyrians are the third largest ethnic group in both Iraq and Syria with communities in Turkey, Iran, Lebanon and other Middle Eastern countries, whose borders were created less than 100 years ago.[4] Today's Assyrians remain stateless and a large number have left their homeland due to both ethnic and religious persecution.

In order to fully understand the plight and perseverance of the Assyrians of Kharput, one must take a brief look at the emergence of the Assyrians from antiquity, and their evolution into the modern era.

---

[4]Agnes Korbani, The Political Dictionary of the Modern Middle East (Maryland: University Press, 1995), 26.

Chapter 1: Assyrians Past and Present

Modern Assyrians trace their ancestry to the Assyrians of antiquity. Geographically, the Assyrian heartland was located in the northern highlands of the Tigris River, east of the Euphrates, and north of Babylon to the area surrounding Lake Van. As a people, Assyrians see their beginnings parallel to the earliest settlements in the Nineveh Plains and Northern Mountains in what is today's Northern Iraq and Southeastern Turkey, respectively. With the rise of Sargon of Akkad in 2277 B.C. (Šarrū-kīn) the first proto-Assyrian dynasty (Akkadian) is founded interestingly in southern Mesopotamia were the Sumerian and Babylonian peoples were incorporated into Assyrian society. Though his humble origin is obscure, Sargon was of Northern Mesopotamian stock (Assyrian) and raised by peasants.[5] Some stories recount him being sent down the Tigris and reared in Sumer, a parallel, and predecessor of the Biblical story of Moses. His empire stretched from the Mediterranean coast to Elam. He founded merchant colonies all the way to Cappadocia. The Assyrian Empire would expand and contract throughout the centuries until the eventual fall of Nineveh in 612 BC, and Harran in 608 BC.

The current Assyrian year, 6753, dates to the construction of the first temple of Ashur, the ancient god of the Assyrians.

---

[5] Seton Lloyd, The Archaeology of Mesopotamia, (London: Thames and Hudson Ltd, 1984), 137.

"Assyrian hymns pictured a God who ruled as Shepard not only of the Assyrians, but over all peoples and all living things, at a time when Yahweh was still only the God of his own single nation."[6]

Dr. Simo Parpola, Director of the State Archives of Assyria Project in the University of Helsinki, asserts that the Assyrian view of God, "which defined Ashur – 'the only, universal God' – as the totality of gods." He further states that Ashur himself was "beyond human comprehension."[7]

The ancient Assyrians have made many contributions to human civilization. In addition to contributions in the fields of philosophy and theology, as mentioned above, ancient Assyrians devised a system of weights and measures, which benefited trade and commerce, built roads for postal carriers as well as caravans; chariots, siege engines in time of war, and the occasional wandering traveler. The Ashurbanipal Library in the ancient capital at Nineveh documents many of these innovations including: the division of an empire into separate governmental sections, division of the year into months and seasons, and contributions to music, literature, mathematics, astronomy and architecture.[8] They can be found today preserved in museums such as the British Museum in London.

In truth, much of what is known as Greek philosophy and science was rooted in the ancient Assyrian-Babylonian civilization. Plato, Pythagoras and others used much of what they learned from the Near East to further express their ideas on science and mathematics.[9] Amazingly, the "barbarous" mask of militarism and cruelty that has been placed over the Assyrian culture overlooks many of these innovations and accomplishments.

New evidence has caused scholars to reinterpret and reconsider their original conclusions about Assyrian military practices and the old stereotypes of Assyrians as "bloodthirsty barbarians". Indeed the growing body of evidence is causing a shift in Assyriology and what was thought to be fact. Georges Roux points out that although severed heads on pikes were common practice in Assyria, they were also common throughout antiquity. In the Assyrian case,

---

[6] Eva Matthews Sanford, The Mediterranean World in Ancient Times (New York: Ronald Press Company, 1951), 122.

[7] Simo Parpola, Assyrian Prophecies, State Archives of Assyria, vol. 21, (Helsinki University Press, 1997).

[8] Georges Contenau, Everyday Life in Assyria and Babylon, (NY: St. Martins Press, 1954), 228.

[9] H.W. F. Saggs, The Greatness That Was Babylon, (NY: 1962), 420-425.

there was a politically just case for the practice:

> "It must be noted, however, that these atrocities were usually reserved for local princes and their nobles who had revolted and that in contrast with the Israelites, for instance, who exterminated the Amalekites for purely ethno-cultural reasons, the Assyrians never indulged in systematic genocide."[10]

After the fall of the Empire, Assyrians continued to live among the ruins of their forefathers, or, built new towns over the ruins of the ancient cities. Some moved to new cities, and others continued their agrarian lifestyle:

> "The destruction of the Assyrian Empire did not wipe out its population. They were predominantly peasant farmers, and since Assyria contains some of the best wheat land in the Near East, descendants of the Assyrian peasants would, as opportunity permitted, build new villages over the old cities and carry on with agricultural life, remembering traditions of the former cities."[11]

After the advent of Christianity, the Christian Assyrians would continue their traditions, feasts and festivals and adapt them to their new religion. The Fast of Nineveh, the story of Mart Shmuni and her seven children, and also the holiday of *Nusardil* which began as a pagan rite in adoration of Tammuz, were adapted to fit Assyrian Christian customs.

> "The Bible, indeed, came to be a powerful factor in keeping alive the memory of Assyria and particularly of Nineveh."[12]

According to Dr. Simo Parpola, it was easy for the Assyrians to accept Christ, since many of the teachings of early Christianity were invariable with those of Assyrian imperial religion. Asceticism, the theology of the Trinity, and the Mother of God were arguably based on ancient Assyrian spiritual practice.[13] Unfortunately for them, Assyrians soon began centuries of living under the yoke of successive foreign empires.

The new rulers, the Persians, in fact adopted many facets of the ancient

---

[10] Georges Roux, <u>Ancient Iraq</u> 3rd edition, (NY: Penguin Books, 1992), 291.

[11] H.W. F. Saggs, <u>The Might That Was Assyria</u> (England: Sidjwick & Jackson Limited, 1984)

[12] Ibid,.

[13] Simo Parpola "Assyrians after Assyria" Journal of Assyrian Academic Studies, vol. 13 No. 2.

Assyrian civilization. The Persian *Ahura Mazda* was juxtaposed with Ashur and represented by the winged disk of the Assyrian god.[14] Persian rulers also modeled their palaces and their decorations and sculptures after Assyrian architecture. The *lamasu* (winged bull) is perhaps one of the more obvious examples. Interestingly, they also took the two writing systems of the Assyrians: syllabic and alphabetic. The syllabic cuneiform was based directly on Mesopotamian cuneiform, and was used until the adoption of the Aramaic alphabet.

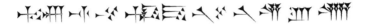

Figure 5. Cuneiform script (read from left to right)

Figure 6. Phonecian/"Aramaic" script (read from right to left)

In Assyria, the cumbersome cuneiform writing system was used by a small number of scribes and religious personnel; the Persian syllabic script was based on this system. Phonecian-Aramaic with its simple alphabet consisting of 22 letters (compared to the more than 800 signs in the cuneiform system, each with several readings and meanings) had already started to replace Akkadian, both as the written and spoken language, by the eighth century B.C.

Why the Assyrians adopted an alphabet seems logical, but a language not their own, is questionable. Was there an actual people and language, which can be classified as Aramean/Aramaic? Modern research is still not quite clear on the matter. Either way, the "Aramaic"[15] problem is far from being solved.

During the Persian Empire, Aramaic became the official language for both governmental and commercial interaction and became the "common tongue" of the East stretching to the Greek region.

In the centuries following the downfall of the Empire, especially in the Christian era, the Assyrians were often called "Syrians", a misnomer stretching back to the Hellenization of the Near East. What the Greeks called "Syrian" referred to what other nations called Assyrian. Dr. Parpola explains,

---

[14] Ibid,.

[15] Please refer to the upcoming article, The Arameans, Aramaic, and the land of Aram: A unified discernable culture, or misunderstood terminology? By S. Donabed.

"The Greek word Syria and the adjectives Syrios and Syros (Συριος, Συρος) derived from it are originally simple phonetic variants of Assyria and Assyrios (Ασσυρια, Ασσυριος), with aphaeresis of the unstressed first syllable."

Indeed, Parpola notes that the dropping of the first syllable is noted in Aramaic sources, and that the Assyria/Syria variants are freely interchanged during the Greek period. Apparently, Strabo unconstrainedly utilized both terms, though they bore the same significance. It is only after the Roman occupation that the terms split and began to take on different meanings.

During the period when much of the Mediterranean and Near East was Hellenized, many Assyrians adopted Greek names, incorporated Greek in their language and studied philosophy with the Stoics, Cynics, and many other major philosophical schools. Though many adopted Hellenistic culture, there were others, who not only did not adopt this new culture but also rebuked it. Notably Luqu (Lucian) of Samosata and Tati (Tatian), retained their Assyrian heritage. To this day, Tatian is best remembered for his <u>Diatesseron</u>[16] composed in classical Syriac in the 3rd century A.D. A student of Justin Martyr, he studied philosophy and was heavily influenced by Greek thought: a fact which seems humorous after one has read his *Oratio adversus Graecos* or Address Against the Greeks, where he explains how the Hellenes owe much of their tradition, art, science, etc. to other peoples who had developed them long before the Greek intellectual movement.[17]

The Assyrian tradition, or more specifically that of the Church of the East and the Church of Antioch, venerate three *Shlihe*[18] above all others. Toma (St. Thomas), Addai (St. Thaddeus), and Mari (St. Bartholomew) were indeed those who brought Christianity to the East. In fact, on the Malabar Coast of India, there are descendents of the Assyrian missionaries, who are called St. Thomas Christians after the apostle who traveled so many leagues to bring Christianity to India.

The Assyrian-speaking churches follow the tradition of Edessa (Oshroene, Urhai/ Urhoi), modern Urfa in Turkey, as the first Christian state, circa 30AD.[19] The legend of Abgar the Black, King of Edessa, and his conversion to Christianity are attested to in Syriac manuscripts. According to the

---

[16] The compiling of the four Gospels into one narrative.

[17] <u>Address of Tatian to the Greeks</u> *(Oratio adversus Graecos)*

[18] Saints

[19] Eusibius, <u>The History of the Church</u> (Penguin: 1965), 60-65.

legend, Abgar was healed of an incurable sickness because of his belief in Christ; and he decreed Christianity as the official religion of his country.[20] This was common in an era when people usually worshiped as their rulers did. Some historians may contend with the fact that Edessa was an Assyrian Kingdom. Oshroene (another name of Edessa), however, seems to be a clear transliteration of the word *Ashuroye* meaning Assyrian.[21]

According to the writings of Mar Addai, he himself refers to Edessa as being inhabited by the Assyrians.[22] Indeed Edessa had a sister Assyrian kingdom that was known as Adiabene (Arbel region in today's North Iraq). While Edessa was situated in the ancient area of Subartu, (Kharput to Tur Abdien region) Adiabene was termed *Athuria* by the Persians, and sat in the midst of the *Assyrian Triangle* made of Nineveh, Ashur and Arbil. It seems that the people of Adiabene continued their ancient Assyrian traditions; as attested to in their celebration of the Akitu (New Year) festival, which was instituted in Edessa, and by the stylization of its king names, like Sennacherib and others. Truly, the Assyrians did not suffer from "historical amnesia".

In the years following, Assyrian Christianity spread through missionary activity, from its native lands, through Persia, India, and on to China and Mongolia. Church of the East (Nestorian) missionaries traveled from the Near East to the Far East with the Bible in hand, preaching the words of Christ. In the area known as Hsian-fu, there is a monument to the "Luminous Religion" known to us as Christianity. In fact, documents state that in 635 AD "Nestorian" Christians in China asked the emperor of the T'ang Dynasty for permission to practice their religion. The emperor agreed, calling the religion, "Ta Ch'in Chiao", or the "Ta Ch'in" religion. The Chinese practitioners of Christianity knew it by a different name.

"They themselves used the name Ching Chiao, Luminous Religion (or illuminating?), and referred to their home church as The Church of the East."[23]

---

[20] St. Thaddeus, "Teaching of Addai" Syriac Manuscript -also- "The Legend of Abgar" The Catholic Encyclopedia, www.newadvent.org/cathen/01042c.htm

[21] Robert Eisenman, James the Brother of Jesus (NY: Penguin1998), 862.

[22] Yusuf Malek, The British Betrayal of the Assyrians (Chicago: The Assyrian National Federation & Assyrian National League of America, 1935), 10.

[23] John M.L. Young, By Foot to China (Tokyo: Radiopress, 1984), http://www.aina.org/byfoot.htm

After many golden years of Assyrian Christian education, art, and philosophy, a new threat entered the Middle East. With the rise of Islam, the Arabs came to dominate and repress the Middle East, replacing the Persian rulers. During this period Assyrians continued to thrive despite the domination of foreign rulers. Monks and scholars studied and wrote works of poetry, theology, science and philosophy in Edessa, Nisibis, and Jundi-Shapur in southwest Persia. In fact, it was through the medium of Assyrian (Syriac) that Greek philosophy was retained and passed on initially to the Arabs and, later, to Spain and Europe, thus igniting the Italian Renaissance.[24] Physicians such as Hunayn bar Ishaq (d. 873 AD) whose text on ophthalmology (950 AD) was the standard textbook in the field for centuries, translated and built upon Greek philosophy and science; initially in Classical Syriac and then into Arabic. The Arab Caliphs even employed Assyrians, such as members of the *Bakht-yashu* ("Happiness of Jesus") family as their personal physicians, and asked them to build medical schools and hospitals in their cities. The Assyrian philosopher, Job of Edessa, developed a physical theory of the Universe that substituted matter with forces.[25] The Assyrian Christian writers therefore contributed much to both Western and Eastern civilization, just as their ancient ancestors had done before them.

Unfortunately the future was to make a drastic turn for the worse, and see a decline in Assyrian prosperity. Born in 1336 AD, Timurlane scourged the Near East, and inflicted horrid deeds upon all the peoples of the Middle East, and the Assyrians were no exception. In 1380 AD, he destroyed Assyrian centers in Mosul, Erbil, Nisibis, Tabriz and Bakerda. Timurlane boasted that he would make Samarkand the capital of all Asia. Instead, he destroyed the trade routes and the Silk Road with his arrogance. As Samuel Moffett states,

"He destroyed but could not plant, tore down, but could not build."

The legacy of Timurlane would have long reaching effects on all of Asia and on the Assyrians specifically.

Following an astonishing era of scholarship and scientific advances, Assyrians were once again suppressed into yet another dark age. High taxes by

---

[24] J.J. Saunders, A History of Medieval Islam (NY: Routledge, 1996 reprinted), 188&193.

[25] Peter BetBasoo, "A Narrative History of Assyrians" Information Booklet of the Assyrian American National Federation 1997 Convention, Detroit (Chicago: Assyrian Academic Society, 1997)

the Muslim rulers, and continued hostility forced the Assyrians to flee to more defensible positions. The next 500 years would witness less scholarship and an increase in persecution and murderous genocide, which led to repeat forced migrations and further decimated a broken people.

During this dark period, the Muslim aggressors destroyed thousands of Assyrian manuscripts and books. They also nearly succeeded in destroying the Assyrians themselves. Unfortunately, the ancestors of those who survived the purge of Timurlane and the successive massacres, saw yet another horror with the coming of the Kurmanji[26] Chieftain, Badr Khan Bey in 1842.[27]

There is very little that comes to us from this period in history. A few works have survived the destruction however. A certain "Nestorian" monk by the name Yonan Tkhomnaia (1832-1886), among many others, wrote extensively in Assyrian during the later part of this dark period. Unfortunately only one of his works survives to this day; a book of poetry titled *Guggi*. It is worthy of sorrow, that the world has lost much knowledge and material from this age.

The Assyrians themselves would split on religious grounds in 1552 AD, which saw the division of the Church of the East and the creation of the Chaldean Catholic Church (A Uniate of Rome).

Because of the repeated persecutions and forced migrations, the Assyrians were now divided into separate and isolated communities. In the Hakkari[28] Mountains of today's extreme Southwest Turkey, Church of the East and Chaldean Catholic Assyrians lived in semi-independent tribes lead by a chief or *malik* who answered only to the Patriarch of the Church of the East. Those of the Nineveh plains (consisting of all sects: "Nestorian", "Jacobite", and "Chaldean") lived a wary existence with their Muslim neighbors. The "Jacobite" Assyrians of Tur Abdien lived difficult lives amidst continued threats by Kurdish and Turkish hostiles. In Mardin, Diarbekir, Urfa, and Kharput, the "Jacobite" and "Chaldean" Assyrians had Arabic and Turkish forced upon them by their oppressive rulers further distancing themselves from their Assyrian

---

[26] Termed Kurds. These mixed ethnic Muslim tribes are not indigenous to Northern Mesopotamia, and sadly, many are even of Assyrian background, being abducted as children and young maidens.

[27] Peter BetBasoo, "A Narrative History of Assyrians" Information Booklet of the Assyrian American National Federation 1997 Convention, Detroit (Chicago: Assyrian Academic Society, 1997)

[28] From the Assyrian *akkare* meaning "farmers"

heritage and identity. The Assyrians of the Urmia Plains were mostly of "Nestorian" tradition until the advent of the Protestant missions of the 1800 and 1900s. Despite all the adversity the Assyrians endured, they managed to survive, fighting to defend themselves and their land. Each region, or village, in its own way developed a way of fighting back and expressing its identity.

The 1700s and 1800s would see hope rekindled in the hearts of the Assyrian people. They fought for their name, their language and their traditions in small but significant ways. All Assyrians used different types of symbolism to express their love for their heritage and traditions. A peculiar type of chanting called *Rawe* was, and is still used by tribes who lived in the mountains in what is today Southeastern Turkey. They held fast to their identity in the strongholds of their highlands, similar to those of Kharput. Those of Hakkari, retained their language and sang their *Rawe* as a form of expression of their identity. Prevalent among the Tkhooma and Tyiari tribes, this particular *Rawe* was sung by the latter.

ܐܠܠܟ، ܒܟܝܐ ܫܝܕܣܐ ܗܘܐ
ܘܠܣܟܝܐ ܒܓܠܝܠܐ ܗܘܐ
ܡܣܘܡ ܐܬܐܣ ܢ ܦܐܝܐ ܗܘܐ [29]

Translation: I Ask for Tyari to be unified,
And for egoism to be ceased,
Perhaps then Assyria will rise.

There remain no precise dates on these chants since they have been orally conveyed, though they are old in the sense that they have been sung for generations dating back hundreds of years.

In 1849, *the Assyrians in Urmia*[30] published *Zahreere d'Bahra* or *"Beams of Light."* It was not only the first newspaper to be published in Iran, but probably in all of Middle East. Its 150th anniversary was celebrated in 1999.

Many people in Kharput made flags, which symbolized Assyrian history. The following explanation was used by the Assyrians of Kharput to explain the various aspects of the their flag.

I am a proud, noble and ancient flag whose colors signify:
Purple for the Royalty of the Empire of Assyria
White for Constancy and Purity
Crimson for the centuries of Assyrian blood sacrificed on the altar of Nationhood and Faith
The three stars on the Royal Purple represent the areas of Nineveh, Babylonia, and Akkad.[31]

These oaths and segments of collective consciousness may seem to be small accomplishments, but for a nation fighting for its survival, they are significant achievements, and indeed were laden with fear of torture and death within the country of the oppressor.

Following the genocide that was carried out against the Assyrians, in 1914-1918 in present-day Turkey, many Assyrians who escaped the horrors, fled the Middle East. Over one million Assyrians met death at the hands of the

---

[29] Gewargis & Khoshaba, ܟܝܢܐ ܐܫܘܪܝܐ ܘܝܐ (Baghdad 1998), 62.

[30] A compound Assyrian term meaning "Place of Water."

[31] Private Collection of Sidon (Saide) Samuel

Ottomans and their cohorts. On the land of their ancestors, the Assyrians fought for survival. In Tur Abdien, particularly in the fortress of Ein Wardo, western Assyrians fought successfully to keep out marauding Kurds. In Mardin and its surrounding villages, the Kurmanjis burned Assyrian women alive in an attempt to find "swallowed gold".[32] In Urmia, Iran, Assyrians fought the brunt of Persian and Kurmanji/Sorani forces under the leadership of *Rabkhayla*[33] Agha Petros, of the Assyrian Hakkari Mountains. In the plains of Nineveh, Assyrians fought for survival in the villages of Alqosh, Tell Kefe, and further north, Ainkawa and Araaden among others. Every Assyrian, of all denominations, had some relative who perished during those terrible times when almost two-thirds of the entire Assyrian population was wiped out.

The Assyrians were promised safe haven and eventually an autonomous state of their own in their ancestral homeland by both the French and British regimes for helping them during the war. However, they were betrayed by their former allies when, at the conclusion of the war, they were disarmed and left to the mercy of the very people they had been fighting. The betrayal was seen by the world, and one can point to the time prior to the establishment of a Jewish state in Palestine for proof of is diffusion into the rest of the world.

Jewish settlers knew all too well of the betrayal of the Assyrians, and were mindful of its implications for their own resettlement of Palestine.

> "You have seen what happened to the Assyrians just as soon as they ceased to be of use to the British. You read how the English minister stood up in their Mejliss at Westminster and disowned any claims made by their fellow Christians, pleading for their wives and children to be safe from rape and slaughter."[34]

The Assyrians encountered betrayal after betrayal from their western "allies." Despite being superb mountain fighters, (compared to the Nepalese Gurka warriors by the British) their numbers were minute and death was felt by the entire nation.

In 1933, 3000 Assyrians met death at the hands of the Iraqi army and Kurds in the village of Simele, Northern Iraq. This was not only an attack against Christians, but on the Assyrian people specifically.

---

[32] For more information see: Thea Halo, <u>Not Even My Name</u>, (NY, Picador, 2000), 285.

[33] "General"

[34] Douglas Duff, <u>Poor Knight's Saddle</u>, (London, Herbet Jenkins, 1938), 150.

"It may be as you say Effendi. We will not argue about it. Tough, may I say, there was no war in sight in 1933 when the Assyrians were being martyred because Britain feared for her oil in Mosul."[35]

All Assyrians, regardless of their tribe or church affiliation met death on that dismal day of August 7th 1933. The Simele massacre also became a turning point for the Assyrians in the United States, who established this date, August 7th, as a remembrance day for all Assyrian martyrs, known today as *Shawa'a B' Tabakh*.

Through these massacres and betrayals, Assyrians became painfully aware of how they would be treated in the decades to follow. In the past century, ethnic cleansing and Islamization cost the Assyrians highly, in loss of life and property.

Until very recently, Assyrians were unable to teach their language in schools in their ancestral homeland, Iraq. In much of the Middle East, they are seen as either Christian Arabs or Christian Kurds, and unable to practice their culture, religion, speak their language, and have schools; all which continue to purge their ethnicity and religion. Some or, a few political movements have developed over the recent years, working to secure rights as the indigenous people of Mesopotamia. The three most prominent/active groups are:

Mtakasto   The Assyrian Democratic Organization (ADO)
Established 1957

Khuyada Teeweelaya   The Assyrian Universal Alliance (AUA)
Established 1968

Zowaa   The Assyrian Democratic Movement (ADM)
Established 1979

One advantage of living in a Diaspora is the ability, (e.g. the freedom) to produce literature, books and magazines. Some examples are, *Huyodo* magazine published in Sweden, *Nineveh* published in Berkeley, *Renyo Hiro* published in Belgium, *Bahra* newspaper of the ADM, *Darbo* and *Furkono* of the ADO and GFA respectively, and the *Assyrian Star* printed by the Assyrian American National Federation in Chicago.

Many ancient rituals live on within the community until now. For example, *Nusardil*, the "water holiday," an ancient Assyrian practice, was incorporated into Christianity after the Assyrians became Christian. Originally, the ancients threw a water-filled vase upon their roofs at the onset of winter asking for the god Tammuz's quick return from the netherworld and the advent

---

[35] Ibid., 151.

of spring. Christian Assyrians perform this ritual, where they sprinkle water on each other, to signify the baptism of thousands when Jesus threw water upon them during Pentecost.

Zawyakha d' Nisan (Festival of Spring) is perhaps the most important ritual. The celebration of the Assyrian New Year is an ancient festival practiced by the Assyrians to welcome the rebirth of vegetation and new life, inherent in springtime.[36] This was the same Akitu festival practiced in ancient Nineveh by their brethren.

Folk songs, some of divine praise, others of celebration, and some ritualized war marches are among the oldest continuous cultural connections to ancient Assyrians that their modern descendants have today. Sheikhani, Goobareh, Bablekeh, Balatee, Halay, Tamzara and Hago are a few of the 73 identified forms of Assyrian Dances.[37]

All of these traditions are extremely important to the continuity of the Assyrian heritage. In their simplicity and universality, song and dance attract Assyrians from all over the world, with different tribal and church affiliations and allow them to share in a common tradition.

This was clearly how it was in the village of Kharput as well. It shared many of the traditions and institutions common to all Assyrians, yet remained aloof of much due to the fact that it was situated relatively far from other Assyrian communities. The next largest Assyrian population closest to Kharput was situated in Omid (Diarbekir) in the South, approximately one hundred miles away.

There are some differences among the Assyrians living in different regions, many of which may have lived in isolation, separated from other Assyrian communities for many centuries. This includes modifications in dress, in church affiliation, and the dialect of modern Assyrian they speak. These differences are important source materials when dealing with a community, which has been divided and cut off from itself for a long time as a result of repeated migrations due to ethnic and religious persecution.

Though they lost their language and adopted Turkish and Armenian, the Kharput Assyrians remained a separate and distinct ethnic group.

"Their common language in the district is Turkish, in which language it is that the *Athour* of the Syriac and Arabic is converted to *Asour*, and the *Athouri* of the Arabic, (Syriac, *Othoroyo*,) into *Asouri*, the common name of the

---

[36] "Assyria Online", www.aina.org/aol/

[37] Longden & Weikart, <u>Cultures and Styling in Folk Dance</u>, (High/ Scope: MI: 1996), 58.

Syrians."[38]

Horatio Southgate comments on his surprise to find so large a community far separated from the rest of their Assyrian brethren in central Mesopotamia.
He states that the Assyrians of Kharput were only a continuation of the Assyrians of northeastern Assyria, and not, "as I had first supposed, emigrants from the South."[39]

The Assyrians of Kharput were among many Assyrians who retained their identity almost miraculously when one considers the bear minimum with which they had to work. When they arrived in the Eastern US, they created a church and social groups as a community along with other amazing individual work. They were pioneers for the Assyrian people, yet their story has been shaded by old musty bookcases and confined to the lips and hearts of those who lived the tale. Thus we begin the journey from Kharput.

Note 1: The terms, "Jacobite", "Chaldean", and "Nestorian" are only used for means of differentiation; to point out specific details about each group. However, they all remain Christian sects of the Assyrian people.

Note 2: The words Assyrian and Syriac are used interchangeably as to denote the language spoken by today's descendents of the Ancient Assyrians. Although both Aramaic and Akkadian in character, the modern spoken tongue, in its various dialects, is a direct link of over 2500 years into the past.

Note 3: The modern Assyrian tongue consists of two slightly distinct dialects, and various sub-dialects within the two. Though the Assyrians of Kharput would have used western Assyrian prior to the loss of language, both dialects will be used in this book for explanations and examples.

---

[38] Horatio Southgate, <u>Narrative of a Visit to the Syrian Church of Mesopotamia</u>, (New York: 1844), 87.

[39] Horatio Southgate, Narrative of a Visit to the Syrian Church of Mesopotamia, (New York: 1844), 81.

Chapter 2: Town Life

The Town

Ragozin in his The Story of Assyria states that *Kar* means fortress[40]; and according to Dr. H. M. Deranian, the Assyrians called the village Paght.[41] It seems more likely that the name of *Kar* for Fortress was used in conjunction with *patu* for Open; thus "Open Fortress." In modern Assyrian, it is spelled

ܟܪܬܐ or ܟܪܬܐ. A dot under the kap/kof makes the sound a *kh* as in the Scottish *loch*, rather than a soft *k* as in keep. Although this is the main spelling, there are other variations as well. One may also find it as ܟܪܬܐ and various other spellings.

Kharput lies within the district of Elazig at the summit of the highlands of the South Eastern Anatolian plateau. The province of Kharput was divided into two separate sections. The two provinces, known as Ulova and Kuzova, contained over 300 villages and towns in their vicinity. The provinces of Sivas, Erzurum, Diarbekir, and Halab border the town of Kharput. The town is approximately a two-hour drive from the city of Diarbekir through mountainous terrain; thus one may well imagine the difficulty of travel before the advent of the automobile. Yet despite these obstacles, the people of the area were quite resourceful.

Given that Kharput lay on the border of the Assyrian Empire, the

---

[40] Zenaide A. Ragozin, The Story of Assyria (New York: The Knickerbocker Press, 1887), 262.

[41] Marderos Deranian, Hussenig, (Worcester, MA: 1994 translation by Dr. H.M. Deranian), 7.

Urartians and the Hurrians may have periodically occupied it. During the Turkish period, Cubuk Bey eventually conquered Kharput in 1085 AD. In 1114 by Artukogollari following the Malazgirt War, Anatolian Seljucks in 1234, Ilhanlilar in 1243, Dulkadirogullari in 1363, Akkoyunlular in 1465, and finally the Ottomans in 1516. Most of these overlords meant little to the towns-folk and village people, seeing the Kurds as more of a threat to their remote habitat. Thus Kharput, although also meaning a large area in Ottoman times as the Willayet of Al-Aziz, is today referred to specifically as the ruined town above the city of Elazig.

Kharput sits at the pinnacle of a mountainous highland about four thousand feet above sea level.[42] The topography of Northern Mesopotamia is quite mountainous. A picturesque setting gives the onlooker a vision of a summer resort. Adjacent to the town stood the ruins of an old fortress with ancient pillars.

There are many theories as to who built the fortress and when it was built. Dr. James Barton, the second president of Euphrates College, stated that a forgotten race had built the citadel over 8,000 years ago. Dr. Deranian, in his book Hussenig, states, "According to the inscriptions, a people called the "Jenatsis" built the fortress."[43] As of 2003, there are no visible inscriptions left on the fortress. Yet, there do appear to be some drawings of animals, which remain intact, although faded, upon the walls. Today much of the fortress remains in ruins, and any non-Ottoman inscriptions have been removed.

Armenian writer H.M. Deranian believes that the Assyrians may be the original inhabitants of the town, and the dating of the Assyrian Church of the Virgin Mary's consecration in 179 A.D. supports that hypothesis. The Assyrians of Kharput assert that they have lived there for centuries as frontiersmen, traders, miners, and metallurgists, from the time of the Assyrian colonies in the land called Subartu on the northern boundary of Assyria. It is very probable that the town existed as an Assyrian outpost between the heartland and the merchant colonies in Cappadocia.

Many natural wonders make Kharput and the surrounding area a treasure for adventurers. Approximately eighteen kilometers outside the village is the Golan Thermal Spring in Krakocan. Its forty-five degree water is said to be useful for many ailments, including liver, skin, gall bladder, intestinal, rheumatic and gynecological infirmities. There are many other mineral spas in the area, known too for their healing properties; Yurtbasi Bitter Water and the

---

[42] Leslie A. Davis, The Slaughterhouse Province, (NY: 1989, Aristide D. Caratzas), 38.

[43] Marderos Deranian, Hussenig, (Worcester, MA: 1994 translation by Dr. H.M. Deranian), 5.

Harput Dabakhane Water among the most famous. According to legend, the grave of the original Santa Claus is also in the immediate area; quite possible when oral tradition points to his work in Kharput, Malatyia and the surrounding areas.

At the time within which this book is concerned, houses filled the hillside from east to west. During the period of 1915-1918, there were approximately 30,000 people living in the area of Kharput.[44] Without the church records, it is difficult to know the exact Assyrian population. In addition, most of the Assyrian population, due to speaking Armenian and Turkish, were included as part of the Armenian Millet (Church-Nation) under the Ottomans. Yet, although they had recognition problems, the Assyrians lived despite hostile conditions and provided for themselves and their families. It was not uncommon for Assyrians to travel hundreds of miles in various directions offering goods and services.

---

[44] Leslie A. Davis, The Slaughterhouse Province, (NY: 1989, Aristide D. Caratzas), 38.

Figure 4. Kharput Circa 1910. View from the north east.

Figure 5. Kharput Circa 1910.

Agriculture was the most profitable occupation in the area. A thousand feet below the city was a fertile plain where many farmers made their living. Within the town itself, farming was less than hospitable. The soil was rocky and unfit for raising crops. Some farmers lived in the area, though many had since long moved to the town of Malatiya 30 miles away, where the soil was better, or to the rich soil of the Elazig region, about an hour's walk down the mountain.

There were a variety of animals in the area. Men found hunting deer in the surrounding hills a simpler way of producing a nightly dinner. Few people kept cows, as they were large, and space and food were very limited. Most kept sheep for wool and meat. Chickens were very prevalent and they needed less room to roam about, and most were kept in small pens. Goats were important, their milk used for drinking and to make cheese and yogurt. Donkeys were the beasts of burden, carrying heavy loads, traversing the rocky area. Some families kept cats and dogs as pets, though they always served other purposes, such keeping an area free of mice, and keeping watch on the sheep. Some people kept horses, though it was usually the wealthy that could afford the expense of its care. Horse and buggy was perhaps the best way to travel, though few could afford the luxury.

High up along the cliffs waterfalls were prevalent, especially after the winter season and the advent of the first rains of spring. There were also many natural springs in the mountains, one of which had a bathhouse built near it. About thirty-forty feet away from the church was an inlet stream of the Euphrates. It was used for washing clothes, pots and pans, and further down the river, people cleaned animals before cooking them. The bathroom was farther down the stream, as not to contaminate the clean mountain spring water.

Along the northeast side of the church sat an oval, 150 feet by 50 feet. It was a large graveyard, a holy burial ground for hundreds of generations of Assyrian family plots. Red dirt is now all that remains of a once ancient graveyard of the Assyrians. All the headstones, which were once remembrances of ancestors long dead, chiseled upon by generations of bishops, are all gone, stolen by thieves and eventually used for other purposes by the Turkish government.[45] In fact it is quite common that new settlers or squatters to the area would use old artifacts (stone, brick, etc.) as pieces of their uncomplicated dwellings.

---

[45] Kasper Safer, Oral Interview, February 2000.

Figure 7. Kharput Circa 1914

Figure 8. A view of Kharput from the west. (circa 1912)

According to author Diana Drake, about 100 years ago, Kharput had over 800 shops, 10 religious schools, 8 churches, many libraries, inns, and bathhouses. She states that earthquakes were the main reason much of its population had left the area for the city of Elazig. Of course, one cannot discount that the *massacre of the Assyrians* had something to do with the lack of population as well. Most of the buildings and their objects were destroyed or stolen during and after WWI.

Despite loosing its populace, one would assume some remnants and artifacts would have remained intact. This was not the case since Kurdish bandits rampaged the area on a regular basis. The one ancient artifact from pre-Christian times was that of a horse statue that stood outside near the gate of the village.[46] In the year 1973, the statue unfortunately disappeared. A local man of Malatiya, Napoleon Markarian, remembered seeing the statue when he was a young man. However, when Mr. Kasper Safer went for a visit in the early 1973, there was no trace of the statue. As of 2003 there is no recollection of the statue by any of the inhabitants of the area. Some elders now living in the United States say foreign missionaries were responsible, others declare local thieves, took it. It was one of the last pre-Christian objects left in Kharput.

Caves were found along the hillside. Children were more apt to be wandering in and out of the small spaces. Many received nasty surprises as many snakes tended to reside within the solitary confines of these caves. There seems to be some dispute over the abundance of trees in the village. Prior to 1925, there may have been various sections of short trees and shrubs especially along the streambed, however, after 1970, most have been cut down.

The hills around Kharput were also known for their concentrations of

---

[46] Sidon (Saide) Samuel, Oral Interview, Autumn: 1999.

iron ore. The Assyrians of Kharput affirmed that their ancestors were merchants in the mountains of Subartu, trading with the motherland. They had built for themselves a village outpost or fortress at the zenith of a mountain, which would be easily defensible.[47]

---

[47] Ibid.

The People & Daily Life

When British historian/travel journalist Horatio Southgate visited the region in the mid 1800s, he stated there were about 150 Assyrian families in Kharput. This though was not reliable, as they quite often made their numbers smaller as not to attract the Turkish government's attention.[48] The population ratio of Assyrians to Armenians seems to have been larger on the Assyrian side, or at least up until WWI.[49] However as stated earlier, since they were hundreds of miles away from the nearest Assyrian center which was Omid (Diarbekir), Assyrians were counted among the Armenian *Millet*. Of course, many were also confused as Armenians, as they had lost the Assyrian language at least a few hundred years prior to the start of the 20th Century.

The Assyrians were termed *Assouri* in the Armenian language, and in Turkish were either *Asuriler* or *Suryani Kadim* (meaning "Old Assyrians"). Travelers to the area and many western historians find these names misleading.

> "At the Armenian village of Arapout, where I stopped for breakfast, I began to make inquiries for the Syrians. The people informed me that there were about one hundred families of them in the town of Kharpout, and a village inhabited by them on the plain. I observed that the Armenians did not know them under the name which I used, *Syriani*; but called them *Assouri*, which struck me more at the moment from its resemblance to our English name Assyrians, from whom they claim their origin, being sons, as they say, of Asshur...[50]

Few Turks lived in the area, and Kurds came every 20-30 years for marauding and thieving purposes. Relationships between the two major groups (Assyrian - Armenian) varied from person to person. Some Assyrians and Armenians intermarried, yet most remained with their own community. There was also a great deal of hatred between the two peoples. Sometimes fights would break out between Armenians and Assyrians within the bathhouses.[51] It

---

[48] Horatio Southgate, <u>Narrative of a Visit to the Syrian Church of Mesopotamia</u>, (New York: 1844), 87.

[49] Sidon (Saide) Samuel, Oral Interview, Autumn: 1999.

[50] Horatio Southgate, <u>Narrative of a Visit to the Syrian Church of Mesopotamia</u>, (New York: 1844), 80.

[51] Kasper Safer, Oral Interview, February: 2000.

was not uncommon to have blood feuds between Assyrian and Armenian families. Some small villages around Kharput were known to raid each other in hopes of extracting revenge, fulfilling debts of honor. Despite all the problems, there was a certain amount of respect and tolerance due to religious similarities and a common enemy in the Muslim rulers.

Among the 300 or so villages in the area, Hussenig was amid those that demonstrated a large Assyrian presence. Along with the Yousef family were the Yoten Aghbranks, Nahigians, Topal Agopenk, Tootoondji Simon, Maloota and others. Although some of these families had Armenian last names (some with the addition of IAN) they were doubtlessly Assyrian. Many went by these Turko-Armenian names, as they were easily recognizable. Assyrians by the name of *Bishara* were known more often as *Avedis*, as the two names are identical in meaning, yet the Armenian became more recognizable as their numbers increased, and cause became aided by western missionaries. Interestingly, the Assyrians retained their distinct ethnicity and identity albeit loosing much of their language.

The main question is why would a small ethnic group decide to remain distinct from the main Christian element in the area? Knowing the Armenians had the backing of various western countries, some Assyrians aided them in their struggles. In fact, the Assyrians suffered largely at the hands of the Muslim and non-Assyrian predators of Northern Mesopotamia for sympathizing with the Armenian movement. Although the Assyrians did not raise arms against the Ottomans in a deliberate act of defiance, they did act to protect themselves from any and all enemies who would do them harm. Thus they fought and died never recognized for the acts of dishonor perpetrated against them.

January 1916 by a missionary in Urmia:

"Today is a wet, shivery, snowy day, the first wintry day we have had, and in every one of the score or more villages round about us are thousands of shivering, naked children huddled close together in dark airless cellars, in stables, in partly enclosed balcony-like places, grateful for a scrap of dry bread. Hundreds are still lying sick with this same dry bread as their only nourishment, and these miserable holes as their only home; until we who have seen so much of it all through this awful year have almost ceased to feel even a pang at the sight of the long rows of graves in the village cemeteries. Personally I feel it a cause for thanksgiving that there are several thousands of less children than there were last New Year to suffer the miseries of hunger, cold, sickness, and exile."[52]

---

[52] William W. Rockwell, Ph.D., The Pitiful Plight of the Assyrian Christians in Persia, (New York, 1916), 24.

Knowledge of such events happening to all Assyrians around the Middle East gave their brethren cause for solidarity. This common suffering gave the Assyrians a common hope, and uncommon courage.

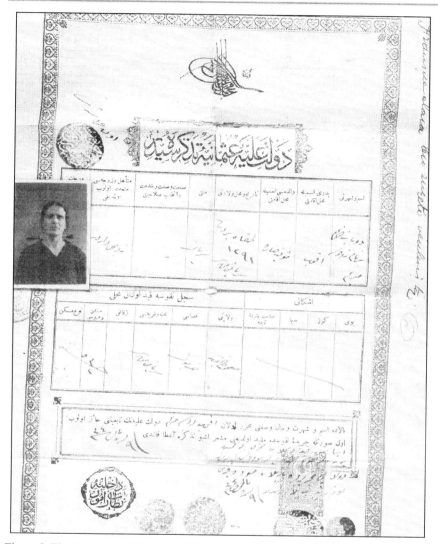

Figure 9. The *Eeqama* or Ottoman residency papers of Miriam Donabed. Notice top box forth from the right states *Suryani Kadim* (in Ottoman Turkish) as ethnicity.

Figure 10. The Ottoman residency papers of an Assyrian, Behnam Donabed.

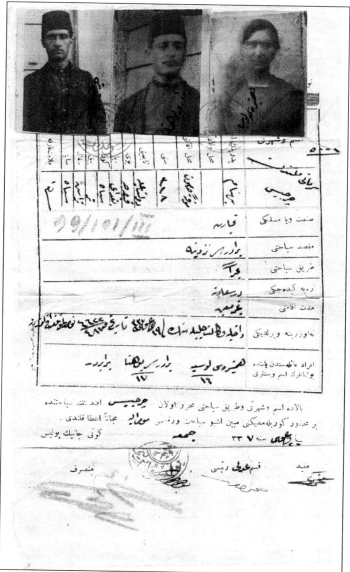

Figure 11. George, Lucy, and Youhana Donabeds' Ottoman Turkish residency papers.

Figure 12. The Donabed (ܐܕ݂ܒܐܢܘܕ) family in Kharput 1920: center Lucy; center right Georgis; center front, Youhana; upper center, Elias.

Figure 13. The Kazar (𐌉𐌓, 𐌓𐌆) family in Kharput circa 1925. Ohan and Anna center. Upper row, Margaret, Roumel.

Each morning before school, Assyrian children would rise with the sun and begin the duties of the day. Many had farm duties to which they had to attend before going to church. Never was there an exception to this. At dawn, as the sun rose in the East and poured light through the one window of St. Mary's Church bathing it in a golden nimbus, voices singing two thousand year old hymns could be heard along the narrow streets of Kharput. From there, most children were off to school, to study their daily lessons, which would be given in Turkish.

The education system of Kharput was relatively well structured for a Turkish school system at the turn of the century. Assyrian children were certainly not lacking in basic education. For some unknown reason, the Assyrian Church hierarchy brought Armenian teachers to teach their children Armenian. Why they did this is uncertain. This angered many people, including, interestingly, some other members of the Church hierarchy.

Hassio[53] Abdenur came from Mardin and saw many Assyrians speaking Armenian. He stated that from that day forth, any Assyrian caught speaking Armenian would be fined; a monetary penalty. Though Kharput Assyrians could not converse in Assyrian, they did understand it too an extent, as visitors from Omid (Diarbekir), Mardin, Urhoi (Urfa), and Midyat were common. Though they had read about Eastern Assyrians (Church of the East), one lady stated she had never encountered one until coming to the United States. There were some "Chaldean" Assyrians in Diarbekir, so they were better known among the "Jacobite" community.

---

[53] "Bishop"

41

Figure 14. The Assyrian School children of Kharput. David Perly #2, Dr. Ashur Yousouf directly above #36 (Circa 1908)

Houses in Kharput sometimes contained 10 to 15 people living under one roof. In some cases there were upwards of 20 people in one house. [54] Many times children would leave to find their own way, not wishing to burden their parents. Some Assyrians went to cities to find work. Mr. Kasper Safer of Worcester, Massachusetts recall's his uncle:

> "He was the first policeman in Constantinople, and he was a Christian Assyrian."

This was truly unique in a time when the Ottoman Turks had much disdain for ethnic minorities, especially the Assyrians, being the true indigenous inhabitants of the area.

There were many prominent Assyrian families in Kharput. The *Dasho* family was known for its wealth, mostly through agriculture. They owned farms upon which Armenian workers would tend to the everyday chores. The *Dashos'* had a reputation for being quite fair with their workers; they split the crop equally with their workers.[55] The *Barsam* family worked as textile and fabric merchants. They went as far as France to buy cloth for trading purposes.[56] Some families were dye merchants, and made a living off colorful cloth for clothing etc. The *Donabeds, Yusufs, Perchs, Safers, Deinhas, Arakels*, and *Barsums* were key families in the Kharput region for trade and craftsmanship.

---

[54] Kasper Safer, Oral Interview, February 2000.

[55] Harold Perch, Oral Interview, February 2000.

[56] Ibid.

The Church

The Church of the Virgin Mary in Kharput was consecrated as a church in 179 AD. It sits under the east face of the mountain overlooking a ravine down below where flows part of the Euphrates River. One legend says that in prior centuries, it stood as a temple to one of the old gods' of Assyria.[57] Another legend, heard by Horatio Southgate during his travels in the area in the early 1800s, states the original church was built by Mor Addai (Saint Thaddeus). It stood as a wonder, with high vaulted ceilings and gold trimmings. It was then destroyed or perhaps fell into disuse, only to be rebuilt by a woman who was known only as Helena. An old priest of Kharput relayed that in the following years during the scourge of the Tartars, Timurlane sacked the Church and stole all of its valuables. Timurlane had assumed that the church walls were embedded with gold, and that fire would melt it free. He then filled the inside with hay and lit a blaze, with the expectation of seeing gold seeping from the walls. He succeeded in only blackening the internal nave.[58] In truth the blackened walls remain today, the church dim and foreboding.

> "One might have thought he was going into a dungeon, so dark and dismal was it, – or rather, dare I say, into some Christian temple of early days, when persecuted followers of Christ worshiped in secret places for fear of their enemies?"[59]

During the 1800s, before one reached the church, he/she walked through an outer gate and a courtyard, finally entering the priest's house. The priest's house contained extra rooms where visiting bishops and pilgrims could stay before returning to their villages (in the near future). Past the priests house stood a low heavy door which lead to a passage. One had to stoop to enter the dark passages, which lead to another massive door, which admitted one into the nook of the church.[60] There was one hole in the roof that was so small adults

---

[57] Leslie S. Thimmig, *"Nineveh"* Magazine, (Berkeley, CA: 1997, Assyrian Foundation of America, Third Quarter vol.20 #3), 4.

[58] Horatio Southgate, <u>Narrative of a Visit to the Syrian Church of Mesopotamia</u>, (New York: 1844), 86.

[59] Ibid, 84.

[60] Ibid, 84.

were unable to crawl through it. It was approximately 2ft by 2ft and lead to the cliff above the town. Children used to play there until it was blocked off so that no intruder could enter the church from above.

The church was very well built. During the summer months it remained cool and in wintertime it was relatively warm.[61] So dark was the inside that a person in the late afternoon would have difficulty making out the internal contents. Our best description of the church from the 18th Century is once again that of Horatio Southgate. He gives us a clear picture of its layout. To the north sat a simple chair and staff of the bishop. In the south was the baptismal stone. Before the east wall was altar, plain and simple. The vessels of sacrifice were poor and humble. Only the light of a torch on the wall allowed the visitor to see in the gloom. Upon the altar sat the New Testament in Assyrian with the date 1892 of the Alexandrian period, which is 311 years older than our own era. Thus it was written around 1581 AD our time. The only natural light that saw the dirt floor of the church was from the small glass window above the altar, touching the Bible in wordless adoration.[62]

Most of the church's floor was still made of but earth and rock. Some curious Assyrians had found small shards of artifacts and pottery in the church, but no complete excavation has ever taken place. Today there are two separate sections of the church. One is much older and was most likely the original pagan worship area. The walls in this area remain black, perhaps a testament to Timurlane's destruction from an earlier era.

Much of the original church artifacts, which were not destroyed or stolen, were moved to various locations for protection. There were at one time some relics on the walls, but from about 1910 on, raiders or soldiers probably plundered the valuables. One of those that remained was the door to the monastery, splendid with Syriac script.

---

[61] Sidon (Saide) Behnam Samuel, Oral Interview, Autumn: 1999.

[62] Horatio Southgate, Narrative of a Visit to the Syrian Church of Mesopotamia, (New York: 1844), 85.

Figure 15. St Mary's Church on the left with residences to the right. (Circa 1913)

Figure 16. The door to the Kharput Assyrian monastary.

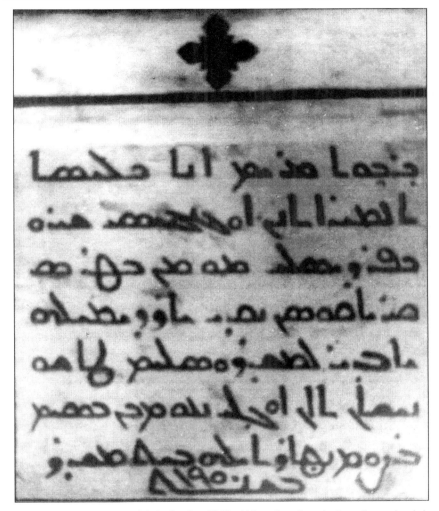

Figure 17. St Mary's Church dedication 1950. Although written in Assyrian script, it is Ottoman in language. Its current location is unknown.

In the mid 1800s, pictures of the crucifixion, Baptism of Christ, and the Virgin Mary could be seen upon entering the church. Horatio Southgate states his amazement to find such icons, as they were not prevalent among the "Syriac-speaking" Churches. He made the assumption that these had been left there by Greek pilgrims who once made use of the church for worship. Among other peoples, the Greeks influenced the "Jacobite" church the most. Indeed, pilgrimages were common to the Church of the Virgin at Kharput, which attracted people from all over the Anatolian Plateau and from all manner of religious backgrounds.[63]

The church was known to be a place of spiritual power. It was known by all the inhabitants of the district of Kharput as a place of healing, a nexus for divine power. The people believed in the power of the Holy Spirit and had faith in the power of Christ. Many western scholars scoff at the claim of miraculous healings that the church people would claim. But people believed, and made their pilgrimages.

Horatio Southgate remains our best picture of what the internal church looked like during the 19th Century. On a huge, immovable stone slab were chains held in place by steal bolts imbedded deep in the rock. There was one inscription in Assyrian that remained on the slab of stone; some say it was gravestone to Helena who built the church on top the previous church built by the Apostle of Christ. Though no one knows for sure. Upon the chain was a collar and manacles to hold the "ill" person. For three days, the person would remain receiving prayers and blessings from the priest. Legend states that a nimbus of divine power would encompass the person and the collar would fall off on its own. Thus this served as a reminder of the healing power of faith.

Ms. Sadie Samuel recalls witnessing such events as a child on her way to school.

> "It was very scary. He was screaming and yelling while they dragged him into the church. Us kids were very scared. But then the same man would be walking around the town a couple days later cured."

It seemed that this healing would cure the nature of any malady. Though, many people, including non-Assyrians, stress that St Mary's was specifically wrought for disorders of the nervous system.

Mr. Kasper Safer remembered the stone from his two visits to Kharput in the early 1970s. He stated that 20ft away from the altar was a rock 6ft long, and probably as deep, covered in Assyrian/Syriac writing. It is possible that the Church itself was built around this rock just as many other early churches were founded around relics and places known for divine occurrences.

---

[63] Sidon (Saide) Behnam Samuel, Oral Interview, Autumn: 1999.

Figure 18. Legends state that the above stone was a gravestone to a local princess who was cured of her ailments by the spiritual powers embodied within the church. Notice the ornate Assyrian rosette in the upper right corner. The text begins by stating, "She left this world...." The rest is mostly worn out and unintelligible.

There was one other stone with Assyrian/Syriac writing still upon it. The inscriptions upon it date back to the expansion of the church in 1135 AD, and state the names of four other Assyrian churches in and around the vicinity of Kharput. Sometime within the past 20 years, the stone found its way to St. George's Assyrian Church in Elazig. Unfortunately, during the rocky wagon ride down from Kharput, the stone split diagonally, leaving it in two halves. Thankfully it is still legible for those students of Syriac to read and use for further research.

Figure 19. The Assyrian stone which describes the expansion of the church in 1135 AD.

Church was central to the lives of the people, although interestingly enough, it was not separate from ethnicity. A testament to this was the Assyrian flag hanging from the ancient church of *Mort Maryam* (St. Mary). A large bell once hung from the top of the church as well. After the exodus from 1915-1920, the bell has since been lost, probably stolen as had been many other objects. In those days, few people could afford clocks, so, as elsewhere, people told time by the sun. The fact that the altar faced east gave early morning churchgoers a comforting feeling as they walked into the normally dank, dark church. It was the central life of the people, and they continued that very tradition when they built St Mary's Assyrian Apostolic Church in Worcester, Massachusetts.

Sacred Music

Since understanding the people and their psyche is extremely important in works containing oral tradition, one must not neglect a small section on music.

Music is an integral part of almost all cultures, and the Kharput Assyrians were no different. During weddings and feasts, deacons would sometimes begin a church hymn or wedding song, eventually to be joined by the rest of the onlookers. There were two types of sacred music to the Assyrians of Kharput: folk music, and religious church music. One such church tune is called *Akh Tagorye*.

> <u>*Akh Tagorye*</u> – Supplication (*takhshifto*) in (*qinto shtithoyo*) the sixth mode
> "Like the merchants, the brave martyrs entered into battle. They shed their blood to obtain spiritual wealth, in the manner of skilled merchants. They bartered their lives for death, preferring torment to rest. They chose death rather than a short life. They are in the kingdom, guests of the son of the King, and we are invited to participate in the feasts, proclaiming 'Glory to Thee, Ruler of the Universe.'"

This hymn remains well-known in the "Jacobite" Church to this day. Within the *Beth Gazo* or Treasury of Chants, a legacy of music can be found. The book is quite large and contains all the various musical modes of the "Syriac Orthodox Church."

Kharput itself had a special type of chanting, a special melody, as did other schools of song within the "Jacobite" Church tradition. Mardin, Takrit (which moved to Nineveh today), Tur Abdien and Diarbekir were among some of the known schools of music situated in Assyrian villages. The music contains 8 modes divided into 8-week cycles. Within each mode there are variants, which depend on the ability of the singer/chanter.

Folk songs were also very common and extremely important to the Assyrians. Since there was contact with Assyrians in other areas of the Ottoman Empire, the people of Kharput knew very well the songs of famous Assyrian Nationalists. Along with their own Dr. Ashur Yousef, *Malphono* Naum Faik of Omid (Diarbekir) was a common name remembered for his writings, poetry, and song.

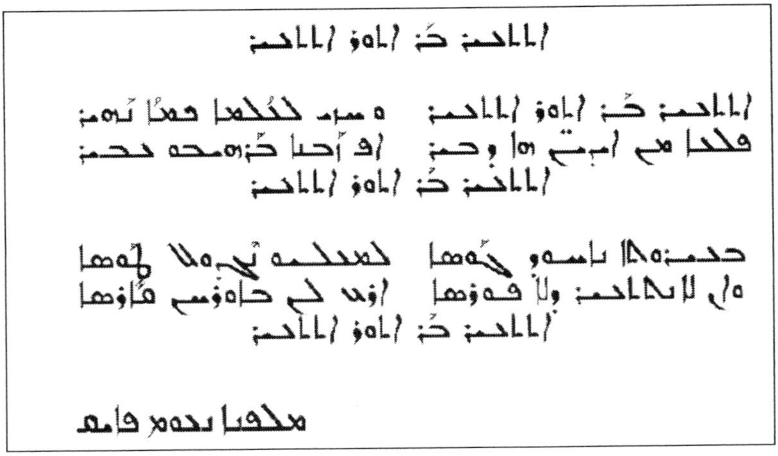

ܐܬܬܥܝܪ ܚܙ݂ ܐܬܘܿܪ ܐܬܬܥܝܪ

ܐܬܬܥܝܪ ܚܙ݂ ܐܬܘܿܪ ܐܬܬܥܝܪ   ܘ ܣܝ݂ ܠܥܠܡܐ ܟܡܐ ܢܗܝܪ
ܦܠܚܐ ܡܢ ܐܝܕܢ ܗܐ ܘܚܙܝ   ܐܘ ܐܚܐ ܚ݂ܘܡܚܗ ܠܚܙܝ
ܐܬܬܥܝܪ ܚܙ݂ ܐܬܘܿܪ ܐܬܬܥܝܪ

ܚܡܚܝܘܐܐ ܒܐܡܣܘ ܘܚܘܡܐ   ܠܚܕܠܚܗ ܢܝܙܘܐܐ ܠܝ݂ܗܡܐ
ܘܐܢ ܠܐ ܢܬܬܥܝܪ ܘܠܐ ܦܘܙܗܡܐ   ܐܘܢ ܠܝ ܚܐܘܢܣܝ ܦܐܘܢܗܡܐ
ܐܬܬܥܝܪ ܚܙ݂ ܐܬܘܿܪ ܐܬܬܥܝܪ

ܢܐܘܡ ܦܐܝܩ

Figure 20. Poem "Awake Son of Assyria, Awake!" by Malphono Naum Faik written circa 1920. Translation: "Awake Son of Assyria, Awake and see the world how enlightened. The chance is fleeing from us, and time is running out. Awake son of Assyria, Awake! In vengeance you will take refuge. Rise up and band together to strengthen. And if one does not awake we have lost our chance. Without a purpose, misfortune will befall our land."

Figure 21. *Malphono* Naum Faik

Religion and Faith

The Assyrians of Kharput had many traditional observances. One of the remembrances was that of *Baoutho d'Ninwoye*, or The Rogation of the Ninevites, which traditionally occurred from Monday to Wednesday of the third week prior to Lent. The fast is done in remembrance of the Assyrians who fasted at the word of God brought to them by the prophet Jonah. The Assyrians of Kharput would fast for three days and three nights, abstaining from eating anything. Each night during the fast, the abstainer would also say supplications in remembrance of God's mercy. This becomes very difficult during work hours. After the third day, those who have fasted usually attend church to receive the *Qurbono*, or Eucharist. This Fast is unique to the Assyrian Christians, and those Oriental Christians whom they have influenced.

Of course, the two biggest religious celebrations were *Qiyimto d'Moran* (Easter), which included a 50-day lent, and *Mawlodo d'Moran* (Christmas), which consisted of a 24 day fast. During these days, people would visit one another everyday. As with many cultures, the holidays were times of family, friends, and essentially togetherness.[64] *Yawmo d' Mort Maryam* (St Mary's Day) occurs on August 15, however it is usually precluded by a week of fasting from animal products. Another traditional saint's remembrance is that of *Shamoun Sobo* or Saint Simon. *Mor Gewargis* (St George) was another saint's day that was ritually observed by the Assyrians of Kharput.

There were also superstitions and spells that some people were known to experiment with in order to protect themselves or to ward off evil spirits. Many Middle Eastern cultures have a ward against the evil eye. Assyrians and Armenians of Kharput alike used this bauble as protection from the greedy, lustful and envious looks of others. There were also people who dabbled in spells of sorts; or perhaps curses are a better term. A spell would be written and then burnt. In a bag were placed the ashes of the paper along with some trinket of value. Essentially the spell would curse those that stole or attempted to steal the object in the bag.[65] This was not uncommon, nor was it widely publicized.

Observances for the dead were also most interesting in comparison with today's practices. The embalming process began with the dead body first bathed and then wrapped in white cloth with salt to preserve the flesh.[66] Then it

---

[64] Sidon (Saide) Behnam Samuel, Oral Interview, Autumn: 1999

[65] George Donabed, Oral Interview "Questions of Childhood Remembrances", Winter: 2000.

[66] Sidon (Saide) Behnam Samuel, Oral Interview, Autumn: 1999

was taken to church at night where the priest would chant hymns for the dead with family and friends. There it would stay overnight awaiting burial. The following morning the body was placed in a simple wooden box and taken to the cemetery where it would reunite with the bodies of its ancestors for millennia in the "red earth" of Kharput.

Chapter 3: Dispersion

Figure 22. Forced deportations of Christians from Kharput.

Before World War I

In the early 1880s, Assyrians left the village of Kharput due to persecution as well as economic problems. It must be noted here that the economic conditions were much worse for the Christians than for the Muslims. Assyrians would not have left any of their towns and villages were they not an easy target for hate crimes and discrimination. Being both Assyrian and Christian, the people of Kharput were forced out to make a life elsewhere. Like many other immigrants who faced such persecution, many attempted the long trek to America.

One of the first Assyrians to come to the United States was Mr. Aharon Safer. In the 1890s, he left Kharput as a young child, with his father and brother. The first obstacle that stood in their way was the problem of getting to Istanbul in order to obtain ship passage to the United States. They traveled the only way they knew how, by foot.

Being led by his father, young Aharon Safer and his brother Charlie began the long trek from Kharput to Istanbul, far west of Turkey. They packed rations, as the trip would be no less than 2 months. One of the main problems they faced besides malnutrition and dehydration was the ever-present threat of hostile Turks and Kurds. They realized that Kharput was relatively safe high atop the mountain, and as Christians, walking across Turkey at that time was quite a courageous feat. They ran during the hot day and hid from marauding bands of Kurds at night. On one occasion while hiding away at night, the pair hid in a pit of stone stairs leading to some underground cavern. Such places were not uncommon, as Anatolia is known for its many historical sites.

Along the treacherous paths the Safer's found sustenance by eating the fruit of the many wild berry bushes in the area. Eventually they concluded the hazardous journey and arrived in Istanbul where they would wait for passage to America. Charlie and his father decided to stay in Istanbul where Charlie became the first policeman in the city. They had made it through much difficulty, and each carried the burden of awareness within them. In truth, the experience gave young Aharon Safer certain toughness, which would become part of his personality later in life.

During the 1890s, there were 5 Assyrian men who lived together in Worcester, Massachusetts, working hard to bring their families over from Kharput. Aharon Safer was the first Assyrian or Armenian in Watertown, Massachusetts. Today, Watertown is known as a major Armenian metropolis; in the early 1900s, it was just another small town in New England. As a young adult, Safer began working to earn money for both himself and his family. He worked for many years at Hood Rubber making shoes for about $40 a week. In those days most people made only $2 or $3 a week.[67] He showed both skill and determination, as it was unusual for a foreigner to make so much so quickly.

In addition, Aharon was known for his brut strength and for (interestingly) his police record due to his many fights at local pubs. According to his son Kasper, Aharon would always knock out the lights first as he was usually alone, and hoping to through his attackers into confusion. One occasion he was hit over the head with a broken bottle and lay in serious condition. As it happens, Dr. A. K. Yousef of Kharput was the Assyrian doctor who saved his life, something Aharon Safer never forgot.

---

[67] Kasper Safer, Oral Interview, February: 2000.

After Aharon Safer was married, he was known for helping his Assyrian people who had come to the United States, and continued sending money to those left in Turkey. As part of his personal possessions, his most prized was his dagger, which he always carried. He used it as a sign of trust when another would ask for help, monetary or otherwise. He would give them the dagger and bid them go to his wife and ask for money, supplies etc. She knew that whoever had the dagger was deemed a friend in her husband's eyes, and would offer her help.[68] It would become evident that Mr. Aharon Safer was a primordial character for later Kharput Assyrians who reached New England.

---

[68] Ibid.

Figure 23. The Safer family. Aharon Safer seated in the center Circa 1917

World War I

Although some Assyrians immigrated prior to the war, the majority was propelled out of Kharput between 1915-1925. On Saturday June 28th, 1915 it was publicly announced that all Armenians and Assyrians were to leave within five days.[69] In the chaos the people packed up what they could and saved what precious valuables they could carry with them. Parents and children leaving all they had ever known behind began the trek from Kharput. Families were sometimes split up, some sent towards Urfa, and others all the way to Istanbul. In either case, the trip would be most difficult in that horses and wagons were in very limited supply.

Those Assyrians sent towards Urfa were less lucky. Mid June in Southeastern Anatolia is relatively torrid, and there is marginal water and vegetation. Some women and children rode donkeys, as they were more abundant, some even had oxen carry their loads, but the majority walked on foot. The journey was long and slow leaving the people open to being robbed and murdered by Kurds along the way. Interestingly, there were American and English representatives in the area who did nothing but watch the dread deportation take place. One, Mr. Leslie Davis, who was well known to the Armenians in the area, described what occurred during the exodus.

> "It is quite possible that the men will be killed, the more attracted women carried off as slaves, and the other women and children left to perish in the desert. In any case, it is quite certain that all will die in one way or another before they ever reach their destination."[70]

The plight of the Christians of Turkey is an unknown tragedy, and one in which millions were massacred due to their ethnic and religious background. Those Assyrians, Greeks, and Armenians, who were lucky enough to find passage or leave to Istanbul, had a better chance of making it out of Turkey. None-the-less, the routes were always permeated with peril, and many died on those long journeys to a new and safer life.

---

[69] Leslie A. Davis, The Slaughterhouse Province, (NY: 1989, Aristide D. Caratzas), 144.

[70] Ibid, 145.

Travel to America

The word immigrate gives most people the impression of someone leaving a country and going to a foreign one. What is seldom realized is that people rarely go directly from one port of call to another, especially in the days of World War I and the years immediately following. The influx of immigrants to the United States was unparalleled at that time. Assyrians all around the Middle East began seeking passage to the West, and the Assyrians of Kharput were no different.

Normally people would travel to places where relatives or friends usually resided in order to have help when they arrived. For most of the Kharput Assyrians it was New England; but the problem was getting there. Quite often many Assyrians and Armenians waited years to receive passports out of Turkey. Such was the case with the Samuel Family.

Boulous (Favlous) Samuel and his family left Turkey in June of 1926. Born in 1882 in Kharput, he was witness to many atrocities and decided to take his family to the US. Those Assyrians who were lucky enough to escape Kharput before the death marches fled quickly. Barely surviving the massacres, Mr. Samuel lived many years in Palestine and Israel. With one Turkish passport for the entire family in hand, Mr. Samuel, his wife Miriam, sons' Samuel, George and Yaakoub (Jacob), and three daughters Helane, Shmuni and Rachel arrived in Aleppo, Syria at the British embassy on July 26, 1926. August 11th of that same year, the American Consulate in Jerusalem gave the family leave to enter the United States.

Figure 24. Behnam Donabed born in 1870 in Kharput. An example of an immigrant Labor ID card.

Figure 25. The Samuel Family (May 25, 1927)

In the United States, the Samuel family came to live well after much hard work and sacrifice. Favlous Samuel became the first full-time priest of St. Mary's Assyrian Apostolic Church in Worcester, Massachusetts

Not unlike the Samuels' story, Ms. Sidon (Sadie) Donabed (b. 1910 Kharput) is another example of an Assyrian roaming without a home. After traveling from Kharput to Istanbul, she waited there for passage elsewhere. She left Istanbul, Turkey for Greece in July 1929. After she returned to Turkey the following month, she was granted permission to leave promising her arrival in Beirut, Syria September 17, 1929. She remained there with her brother Elias until March 13, 1931 when they were granted permission to leave by boat to Greece for a second time where they would wait for passage to the US at the Greek port of Patras at the American Consulate. This constant roving was and still is a constant theme for Assyrians who have left their homes for the West[71].

---

[71] First hand account of the Assyrian massacres at Kharput: See Appendix.

Various Travel and Immigration Materials

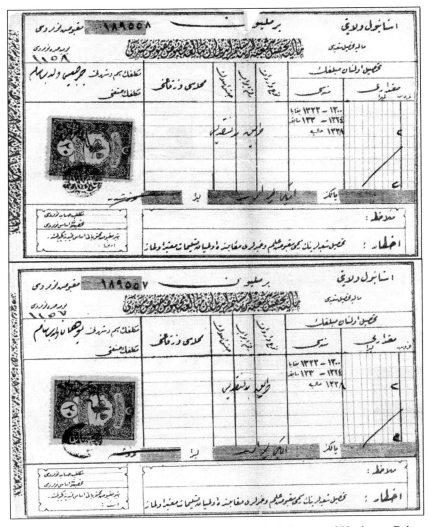

Figure 26. Top document of George Behnam Donabed; Bottom of Youhanna Behnam Donabed. Dealing with travel from Istanbul to Jerusalem.

UNITED STATES OF AMERICA

No.

DECLARATION OF INTENTION

(Invalid for all purposes seven years after the date hereof)

District of Massachusetts | ss: | In the District Court of the United States at Boston

I, Elias Donabed

now residing at 121 School St., Watertown, Middlesex, Mass.,
occupation student, aged 21 years, do declare on oath that my personal description is:
Sex male, color white, complexion brunette, color of eyes brown,
color of hair black, height 5 feet 7 inches; weight 124 pounds; visible distinctive marks none

race Syrian; nationality Turkish
I was born in Harpoot Turkey (Asia Minor), on Sept 1910
I am not married. The name of my wife or husband is

I have not heretofore made a declaration of intention: Number, on

my last foreign residence was Beirut Syria
I emigrated to the United States of America from Beirut Syria
my lawful entry for permanent residence in the United States was at New York on July 7, 1931
under the name of Elias Donabed on the vessel Byron

I will, before being admitted to citizenship, renounce forever all allegiance and fidelity to any foreign prince, potentate, state, or sovereignty, and particularly, by name, to the prince, potentate, state, or sovereignty of which I may be at the time of admission a citizen or subject; I am not an anarchist; I am not a polygamist nor a believer in the practice of polygamy; and it is my intention in good faith to become a citizen of the United States of America and to reside permanently therein; and I certify that the photograph affixed to the duplicate and triplicate hereof is a likeness of me: So HELP ME GOD.

Elias Donabed

Subscribed and sworn to before me in the office of the Clerk of said Court, at Boston, Mass. this 21st day of January anno Domini 19 32 Certification No 1-34944 from the Commissioner of Naturalization showing the lawful entry of the declarant for permanent residence on the date stated above, has been received by me. The photograph affixed to the duplicate and triplicate hereof is a likeness of the declarant.

James S. Allen
Clerk of the U S District Court.

[SEAL]

Form 2202–L–A.
U. S. DEPARTMENT OF LABOR
NATURALIZATION SERVICE

Figure 27. Elias Donabed's Declaration of Intention after entering the United States on June 7, 1931 under the race Assyrian.

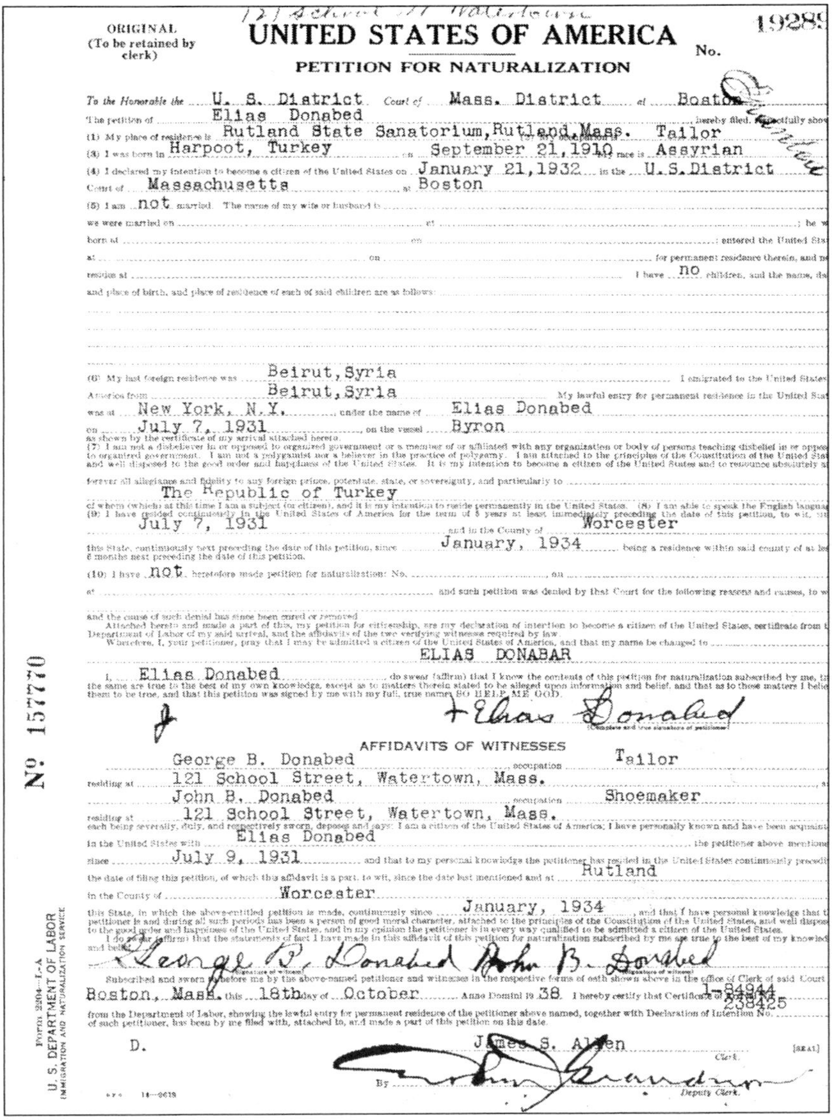

Figure 28. Naturalization Petition for Elias Donabed. Once again with the race filled in as Assyrian. The Assyrians of Kharput were determined to perserve their heritage.

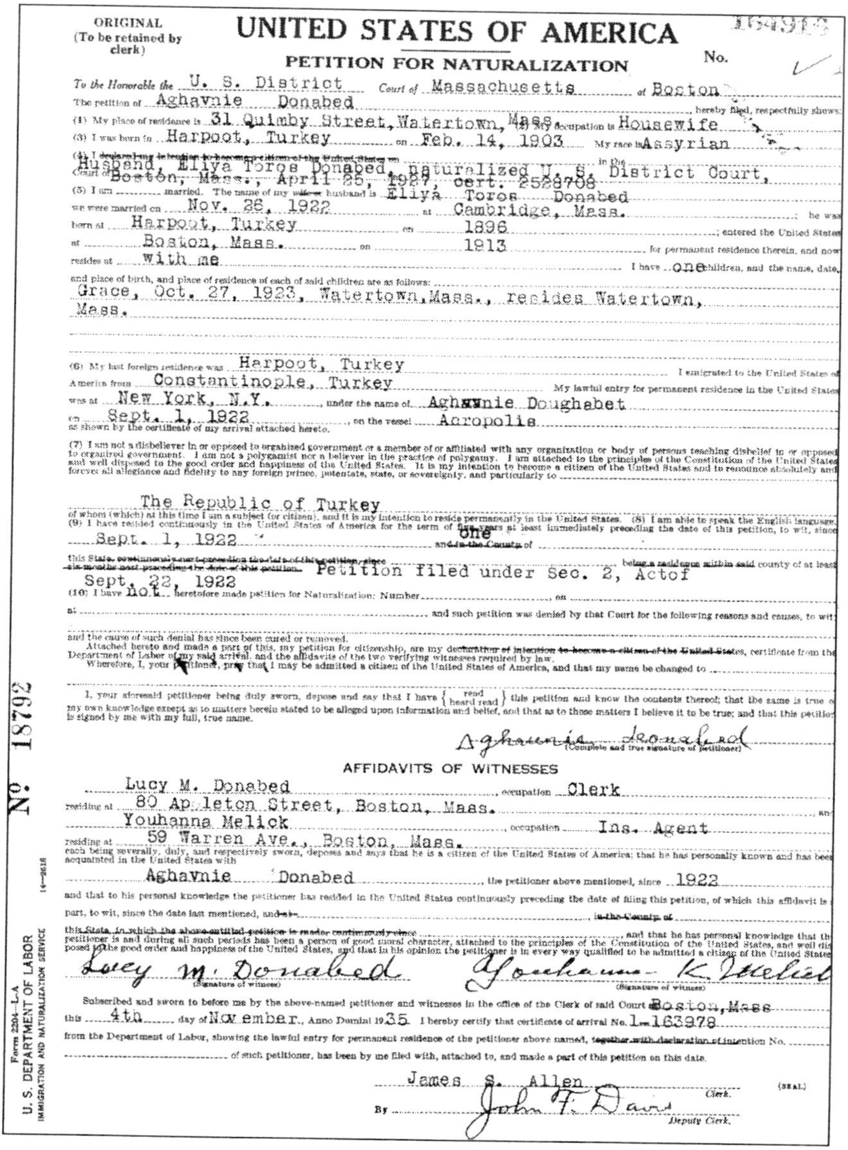

ORIGINAL (To be retained by clerk)

UNITED STATES OF AMERICA

PETITION FOR NATURALIZATION

No. 164916

To the Honorable the U. S. District Court of Massachusetts at Boston

The petition of Aghavnie Donabed hereby filed, respectfully shows:

(1) My place of residence is 31 Quimby Street, Watertown, Mass. (2) My occupation is Housewife

(3) I was born in Harpoot, Turkey on Feb. 14, 1903 My race is Assyrian

(4) I declared my intention to become a citizen of the United States on Husband, Eliya Toros Donabed, naturalized U. S. in the District Court, Court of Boston, Mass., April 25, 1927, cert. 2528708

(5) I am married. The name of my husband is Eliya Toros Donabed we were married on Nov. 26, 1922 at Cambridge, Mass.; he was born at Harpoot, Turkey on 1896; entered the United States at Boston, Mass. on 1913 for permanent residence therein, and now resides at with me. I have one children, and the name, date, and place of birth, and place of residence of each of said children are as follows: Grace, Oct. 27, 1923, Watertown, Mass., resides Watertown, Mass.

(6) My last foreign residence was Harpoot, Turkey. I emigrated to the United States of America from Constantinople, Turkey. My lawful entry for permanent residence in the United States was at New York, N.Y., under the name of Aghavnie Doughabet on Sept. 1, 1922, on the vessel Acropolis as shown by the certificate of my arrival attached hereto.

(7) I am not a disbeliever in or opposed to organized government or a member of or affiliated with any organization or body of persons teaching disbelief in or opposed to organized government. I am not a polygamist nor a believer in the practice of polygamy. I am attached to the principles of the Constitution of the United States and well disposed to the good order and happiness of the United States. It is my intention to become a citizen of the United States and to renounce absolutely and forever all allegiance and fidelity to any foreign prince, potentate, state, or sovereignty, and particularly to The Republic of Turkey of whom (which) at this time I am a subject (or citizen), and it is my intention to reside permanently in the United States. (8) I am able to speak the English language. (9) I have resided continuously in the United States of America for the term of one years at least immediately preceding the date of this petition, to wit, since Sept. 1, 1922 and in the County of this State, continuously next preceding the date of this petition, since being a residence within said county of at least six months next preceding the date of this petition. Petition filed under Sec. 2, Actof Sept. 22, 1922

(10) I have not heretofore made petition for Naturalization: Number on at and such petition was denied by that Court for the following reasons and causes, to wit: and the cause of such denial has since been cured or removed.

Attached hereto and made a part of this, my petition for citizenship, are my declaration of intention to become a citizen of the United States, certificate from the Department of Labor of my said arrival, and the affidavits of the two verifying witnesses required by law.

Wherefore, I, your petitioner, pray that I may be admitted a citizen of the United States of America, and that my name be changed to

I, your aforesaid petitioner being duly sworn, depose and say that I have {read / heard read} this petition and know the contents thereof; that the same is true of my own knowledge except as to matters herein stated to be alleged upon information and belief, and that as to those matters I believe it to be true; and that this petition is signed by me with my full, true name.

Aghavnie Donabed (Complete and true signature of petitioner)

AFFIDAVITS OF WITNESSES

Lucy M. Donabed, occupation Clerk residing at 80 Appleton Street, Boston, Mass. and Youhanna Melick, occupation Ins. Agent residing at 59 Warren Ave., Boston, Mass. each being severally, duly, and respectively sworn, deposes and says that he is a citizen of the United States of America; that he has personally known and has been acquainted in the United States with Aghavnie Donabed, the petitioner above mentioned, since 1922 and that to his personal knowledge the petitioner has resided in the United States continuously preceding the date of filing this petition, of which this affidavit is a part, to wit, since the date last mentioned, and at in the County of this State, in which the above-entitled petition is made, continuously since and that he has personal knowledge that the petitioner is and during all such periods has been a person of good moral character, attached to the principles of the Constitution of the United States, and well disposed to the good order and happiness of the United States, and that in his opinion the petitioner is in every way qualified to be admitted a citizen of the United States.

Lucy M. Donabed (Signature of witness) Youhanna K. Melick (Signature of witness)

Subscribed and sworn to before me by the above-named petitioner and witnesses in the office of the Clerk of said Court Boston, Mass this 4th day of November, Anno Domini 1935. I hereby certify that certificate of arrival No. 1-163978 from the Department of Labor, showing the lawful entry for permanent residence of the petitioner above named, together with declaration of intention No. of such petitioner, has been by me filed with, attached to, and made a part of this petition on this date.

James S. Allen Clerk. (SEAL)

By John F. Davis Deputy Clerk.

Form 2204—L-A U. S. DEPARTMENT OF LABOR IMMIGRATION AND NATURALIZATION SERVICE 14—2618

No. 18792

Figure 29. Aghavnie Donabed's Petition for Naturalization. The *Donabed* name was quite popular in Kharput, as *Shabo* in the Gazertho, and *Nisan* in Hakkari. Note the "race" section in the upper right.

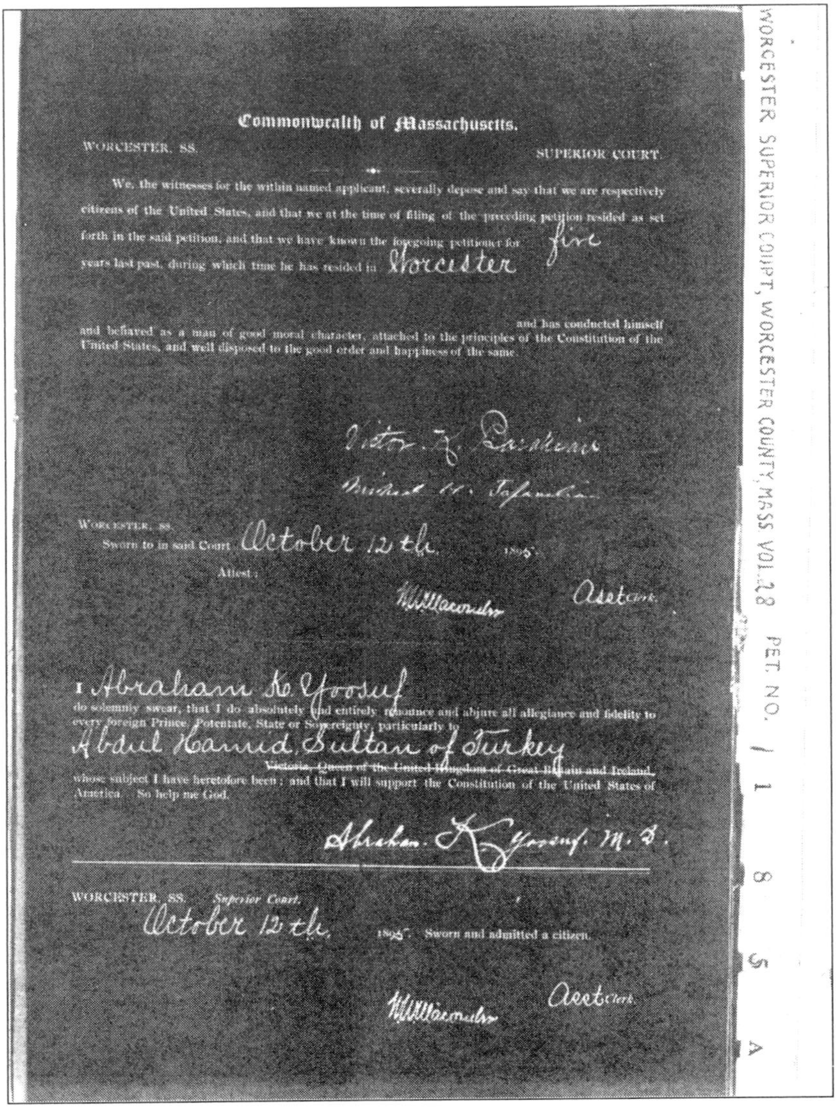

Commonwealth of Massachusetts.

WORCESTER, SS. SUPERIOR COURT.

We, the witnesses for the within named applicant, severally depose and say that we are respectively citizens of the United States, and that we at the time of filing of the preceding petition resided as set forth in the said petition, and that we have known the foregoing petitioner for five years last past, during which time he has resided in Worcester

and has conducted himself and behaved as a man of good moral character, attached to the principles of the Constitution of the United States, and well disposed to the good order and happiness of the same.

Victor Z. [illegible]

Michael W. [illegible]

WORCESTER, SS.

Sworn to in said Court October 12th 1895.

Attest:

[illegible] Asst. Clerk.

I Abraham K. Yoosuf do solemnly swear, that I do absolutely and entirely renounce and abjure all allegiance and fidelity to every foreign Prince, Potentate, State or Sovereignty, particularly to Abdul Hamid Sultan of Turkey ~~Victoria, Queen of the United Kingdom of Great Britain and Ireland,~~ whose subject I have heretofore been; and that I will support the Constitution of the United States of America. So help me God.

Abraham K. Yoosuf. M. D.

WORCESTER, SS. Superior Court.

October 12th 1895. Sworn and admitted a citizen.

[illegible] Asst. Clerk.

WORCESTER SUPERIOR COURT, WORCESTER COUNTY, MASS. VOL. 28 PET. NO. 1 8 5 A

Figure 30. Dr. Abraham K. Yousef's entrance petition to to the United States. (Massachusetts, 1895)

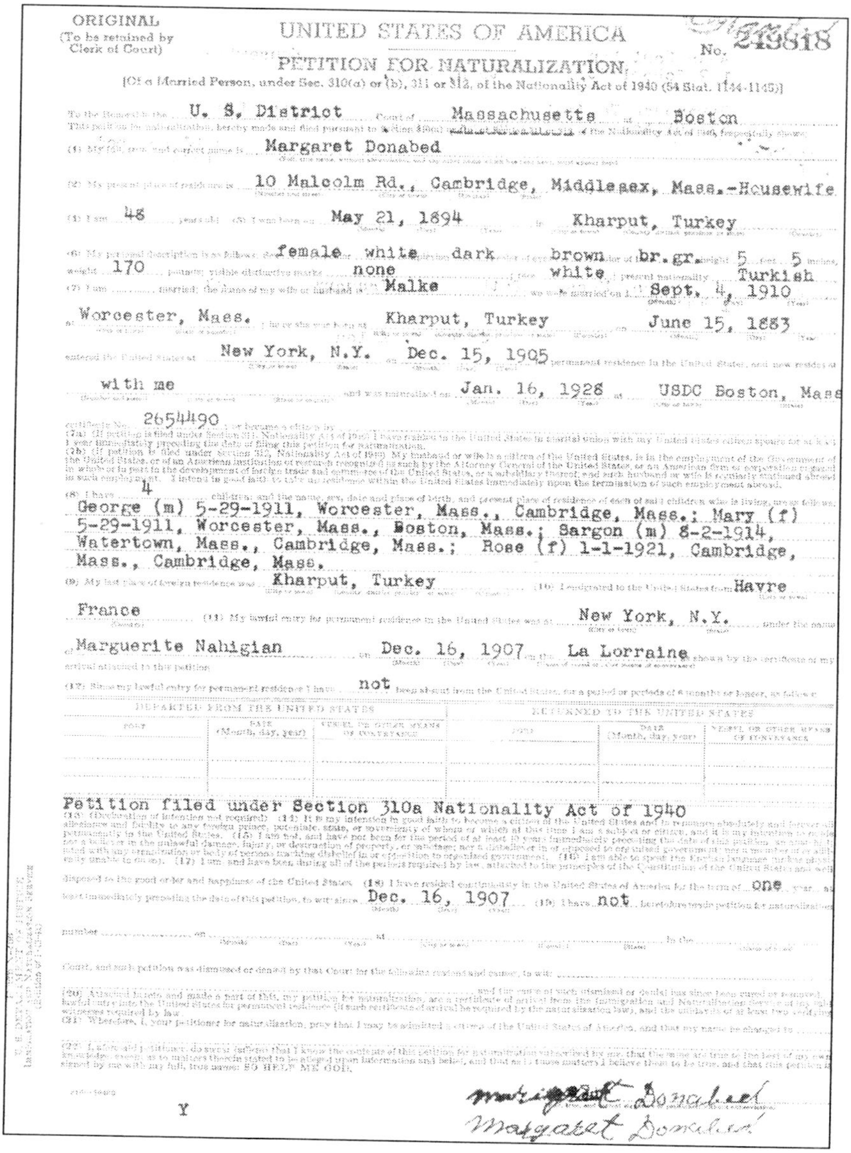

ORIGINAL
(To be retained by Clerk of Court)

UNITED STATES OF AMERICA

No. 219818

PETITION FOR NATURALIZATION

[Of a Married Person, under Sec. 310(a) or (b), 311 or 312, of the Nationality Act of 1940 (54 Stat. 1144-1145)]

To the Honorable the U. S. District Court of Massachusetts at Boston

(1) My full, true, and correct name is Margaret Donabed

(2) My present place of residence is 10 Malcolm Rd., Cambridge, Middlesex, Mass.-Housewife

(3) I am 48 years old. (5) I was born on May 21, 1894 in Kharput, Turkey

(6) My personal description is as follows: female white dark brown br. gr. 5 feet 5 inches, weight 170 pounds, visible distinctive marks none white present nationality Turkish

(7) I am married; the name of my wife or husband is Malke we were married on Sept. 4, 1910 at Worcester, Mass. he or she was born at Kharput, Turkey on June 15, 1883 entered the United States at New York, N.Y. Dec. 15, 1905 for permanent residence in the United States, and now resides at with me and was naturalized on Jan. 16, 1928 at USDC Boston, Mass certificate No. 2654490

(8) I have 4 children; and the name, sex, date and place of birth, and present place of residence of each of said children who is living, are as follows:

George (m) 5-29-1911, Worcester, Mass., Cambridge, Mass.; Mary (f) 5-29-1911, Worcester, Mass., Boston, Mass.; Sargon (m) 8-2-1914, Watertown, Mass., Cambridge, Mass.; Rose (f) 1-1-1921, Cambridge, Mass., Cambridge, Mass.

(9) My last place of foreign residence was Kharput, Turkey (10) I emigrated to the United States from Havre France (11) My lawful entry for permanent residence in the United States was at New York, N.Y. under the name of Marguerite Nahigian on Dec. 16, 1907 on the La Lorraine as shown by the certificate of my arrival attached to this petition.

(12) Since my lawful entry for permanent residence I have not been absent from the United States, for a period or periods of 6 months or longer, as follows:

DEPARTED FROM THE UNITED STATES			RETURNED TO THE UNITED STATES		
PORT	DATE (Month, day, year)	VESSEL OR OTHER MEANS OF CONVEYANCE	PORT	DATE (Month, day, year)	VESSEL OR OTHER MEANS OF CONVEYANCE

Petition filed under Section 310a Nationality Act of 1940

(18) I have resided continuously in the United States of America for the term of one year at least immediately preceding the date of this petition, to wit since Dec. 16, 1907 (19) I have not heretofore made petition for naturalization

(22) I, aforesaid petitioner, do swear (affirm) that I know the contents of this petition for naturalization subscribed by me, that the same are true to the best of my own knowledge ... SO HELP ME GOD.

Y

Margaret Donabed
Margaret Donabed

Figure 31. Margaret Donabed's Petition for Naturalization. Center are names of her children; George, Rose, Mary, and Sargon. NOTE: Ancient Assyrian names like Sargon were common among Kharput Assyrians.

Chapter 4: Establishment in the US

Beginnings

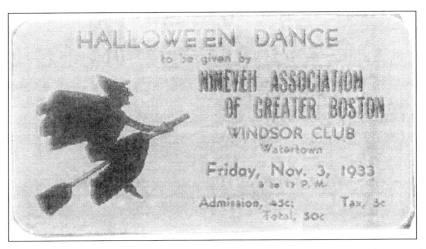

Figure 32. The Nineveh Association of Greater Boston, 1933, halloween dance card.

The Assyrians who immigrated from Kharput began their meetings and societies prior to the formation of a church. Picnics were perhaps the most crucial part of early interaction that the Kharput Assyrians had in the United States prior to an actual club or church. Many picnics were held in the New England area, both in Worcester, Massachusetts and Central Falls, Rhode Island.

When the bulk of the Assyrians had arrived from Kharput to

Massachusetts, they began settling in the cities of Worcester, Watertown, and Lowell, and everywhere in between. These cities were major industrial centers, and immigrants were apt to find promising labor quickly in the factories.

The majority of the community remained in Worcester, Massachusetts and the second highest concentration was in Watertown, Massachusetts. Like many other ethnic groups, they were attracted by work, especially factory work, where getting a job was easy for immigrants who had recently arrived from abroad and did not have a strong grasp of the English language. Some opened up their own businesses after years of hard work. The few who were schooled abroad began studying in college to further their education.

Assyrians then started social clubs and associations to keep the community together and promote the Assyrian language and heritage. The greatest endeavor that the Assyrians of Kharput undertook, as a community newly established, was that of creating a new church.

Figure 33. Assyrians at a picnic Circa 1900 in Rhode Island, with doctor A. K. Yousef standing in the rear. Some names appear to be writtten in by the mother of Phyllis Safer.

Figure 34. Assyrian Kharput picnic early 1900s

- August Picnic -

Sponsored By

UNITED ASSYRIAN ASSOCIATION
of Massachusetts Incorporated

For the Benefit of

MAR APHREM THEOLOGICAL SCHOOL

❖ ❖ ❖ ❖

Sunday, August 12, 1951

CAMP NINEVEH

SHREWSBURY, MASS.

☆ ☆ ☆

Music By

Famous - Harry Hasekian, George Elbag, George Ohan

DELICIOUS ASSYRIAN KAVOORMA & REFRESHMENTS

ADMISSION 50c   Children under 12 Free

NOTE

Buses from Coolidge Square in front of Coolidge Theater, Watertown at 11:30 A.M. $2.00 round trip. Including Admission to Picnic Grounds. Children under 12 - 75c

From Worcester in front of Assyrian St. Mary's Church at Hawley St. at 12:00 noon. Round trip $1.00. Including Admission.

DIRECTIONS

From Met. Boston: Route 9 (Worcester Turnpike) turn left on to Route 20 (Boston Post Road) drive for two miles toward Springfield (Near Hebert's Candy Mansion.)

From Springfield: Take Route 20 - destination two miles before reaching Route 9.

Figure 35. Flyer for an Assyrian picnic on the land purchased and later named Camp Nineveh. The land was reposed by the government under the auspices of eminant domain.

The New Church

Perhaps the most integral part of the Kharput community in the Worcester, Massachusetts's area, was that of the church[72]. Interestingly, there were church organizations before there was a church. The Assyrian Ladies Church Loving Association was organized in 1908, long before the plans for the church had been laid.

In 1923 after many meetings, the Board of Trustees including, Mr. Charles Manoog, Aharon Safer, Beshara Perch, Albert Chavoor, Mrs. Mendoohie Ohan, Mrs. Lucia Donabed, and Dr. Abraham K. Yousef, decided upon a place for the new church. They chose 17 Hawley Street in Worcester, Massachusetts as the home of the church. The land was then purchased for $1200.

In October 1923, the excavation began. In some cases, the people of Kharput came to America with nothing more than the simple clothes they wore. So one can imagine the importance of the new church. August of 1925 marked the beginning of the consecration of Saint Mary's Assyrian Apostolic Church. The Worcester Gazette explained that a high mass and a procession proceeded the laying of the cornerstone. Rev. Naum Koorie, Rev. Nouri Koorie of New York, Rev. Gabriel Boyajy of Springfield, Massachusetts, and deacon G. E. Sugar of Worcester, Massachusetts, packed the faithful into the streets listening to the mass.

---

[72] Past Presidents of the church committee and Priests of Saint Mary's Church: See Appendix.

Figure 36. The grand opening of the completed Saint Mary's Assyrian Apostolic Church in Worcester, MA 1927. The Assyrians of Kharput recognized their national leaders as well as religious; center picture under the American flag is that of Captain Dr. A.K. Yousef with the Assyrian flag on the far right.

Figure 37. The cover of the Assyrian Apostolic Church constitution booklet

That morning, the sermon was preached by Rev. Joel E. Warda (An Eastern Assyrian) of Philadelphia who spoke on "True Christianity" and the work of Assyrians in the role of missionaries from past to present day. Throughout the day and into he evening, people sang and were treated to violin and piano solos from two Assyrians, A. George Hoyen and Anna Hoyen respectively. The treasurer stated the miraculous collection that day resulted in over $1000.

The internal section of the Church was decorated with two pictures of Patriarch Elias III, and *Hassio* Afrem of Damascus. On the outside of the church flew the American flag, and reminiscent of the Church of the Virgin in Kharput, the old purple, white, and red flag of Assyria. Thanks to Phyllis Safer and Harold Perch, we also have a glimpse into the psyche of the Kharput Assyrians of America in the midst of their national pride. According to these two Assyrians, the elder Assyrian women would sew their flags in the church while singing *"Assori yimyez, Assori vortim."*[73]

The church was finally completed in 1927, and about a year later, Archbishop Severius Afrem Barsaum dedicated it on April 22 of that year. During the dedication mass, Rev. Favlos Samuel, Deacon Elias Sugar, and over 40 other deacons assisted *Mor* Severius. This was indeed a momentous occasion for the Kharput people, and one that has never been duplicated since.

While in the area, the Archbishop gave several talks about the Assyrian people and faith. In fact, he was one of the members of the Assyrian delegation, which left to Paris after WWII to request an Assyrian homeland. Ironically the position of the Church with regards to the unity of its people would be drastically altered in the years to come.

Indeed, each and every "Jacobite" Church in the United States was opened with the name Assyrian Apostolic Church of Antioch upon it. After some time, the name was then changed to Assyrian Orthodox Church of Antioch. Eventually every church in the United States, with two exceptions, was changed to Syrian Orthodox Church of Antioch. In the early years of the Church, there was much brotherly activity between The Saint Mary's Church ("Jacobite") and the Saint Thomas Church of the East ("Nestorian") in New Britain, Connecticut. But soon after the changing of the name from Assyrian to "Syrian", little if any interaction took place.

Unfortunately the current church position remains anti-Assyrian (if such a thing makes sense since they themselves are Assyrian) and pro-Arab Bathi, Turkish, and Kurdish. The "Syrian" Orthodox Church today is indeed pro-Middle East governments, and anti-democratic. In fact, a recent vote at a Synod resulted in the banishing of any person calling himself an Assyrian from the hierarchy.

---

[73] The beginning of a song that was sung by Assyrian women in the Armenian language. Roughly translated as: "Assyrian I was born, and Assyrian I will die."

HIS EMINENCE METROPOLITAN · ARCHBISHOP
MAR ATHANASIUS YESHUE SAMUEL

Assyrian Orthodox Archdiocese
OF UNITED STATES OF AMERICA AND CANADA
P. O. BOX 38, WEST NEW YORK, N. J.

August 12, 1952.

My Dear Spiritual Children:

May the Grace of Our Lord Jesus Christ and His Blessing be with you always and keep you under His care.

I have recently been appointed permanently as Patriarchal representative to the United States and Canada by His Holiness our beloved Patriarch Mar Ignatius Aphram I and I am humbly grateful to be appointed your spiritual leader and shall endeavor to fulfill my spiritual obligations to the best of my ability to our churches and its people. I have also been directed by him to establish a diocese headquarters and residence in this country within two years. The location of my headquarters will be decided shortly.

It is my intention to see that our churches are equipped with Sunday Schools, translate certain of our prayers, hymns and history of our church from Syriac to the English so that our younger generation will understand and appreciate our services and thereby increase the attendance of our church so that our ancient Holy religious teachings will be implanted in their hearts and minds.

To see that classes are organized by each priest of our separate parishes to teach our young men the duties of deacons so that they may serve on the altar. I know that our priests will cooperate with me to the best of their ability and I shall give any assistance and advice that is necessary.

To see that our Assyrian people in this country understand their obligations towards the support of our Patriarchate and theological seminary.

It is my purpose to encourage young men with college background to enter into the priesthood so they may be of future use to our churches. These young men could be sent to our theological seminary in Mosul, Iraq, to further their study in our language and our church ritual.

I have already established a new church in Sherbrook, Canada and it is my intention to establish other churches in those communities where our people reside.

I have spent considerable time and have published the catechism and prayer book which has been forwarded to your church and is available to you or I will be very happy to mail you a copy of each upon your request.

The translation of our liturgy to the English is ready for publication as soon as funds are available. After this has been published, it is my desire to continue from time to time, translating other historic or religious books of our fathers.

To do all this, I shall need the cooperation of every Assyrian who has the love of his church and nation in his heart. I shall appreciate any expression from you and hope that you will feel free at all times to communicate with me in all matters that concern our church or the education of our young people.

I extend my blessings to every member of your family.

Athanasius Y. Samuel

Figure 38. Letterhead of the Church prior to the name change.(August 12, 1952)

HIS EMINENCE METROPOLITAN ARCHBISHOP
MAR ATHANASIUS YESHUE SAMUEL

Assyrian Orthodox Archdiocese

OF UNITED STATES OF AMERICA AND CANADA

February 6, 1953

AN OFFICIAL MESSAGE FROM HIS EMINENCE
ARCHBISHOP MAR ATHANASIUS YESHUE SAMUEL

My dear Spiritual Children:

May the Grace of our Lord Jesus Christ be with you and keep you under His guidance.

I feel it necessary at this time to make an official statement about certain rumors that have been circulating concerning the changing of the names of our churches in the United States. I wish to state here, as I have previously stated that I have no intention now or did I ever have any intention of changing the name of any of our churches.

Our churches throughout the world consist of people of many nationalities including those in India, Syria, Iraq, Lebanon, Turkey, Palestine, Egypt, Argentina, Brazil and Chile. These churches are all under the jurisdiction of His Holiness our Patriarch of Antioch and all the East, which carries the name "SURYOYO" "Syrian Patriarch of Antioch" as it has been an established name since the first century A.D.

I have been appointed to represent His Holiness Mar Ephraim I in the United States and Canada and it is my duty to follow His instructions in all matters concerning the church and it is my intention to limit my efforts to those matters pertaining to the church.

It is my sincere wish and humble desire to ask our clergy and all my parishioners to cooperate with me towards building a better religious future for our beloved Assyrian children of this country.

At this time, I shall remind you that it is your sacred obligation to attend our churches if at all possible and your duty to bring your children to our church where they can associate with other Assyrian children and thereby begin to learn the fundamentals of our religion.

I extend my blessings to each and everyone of you.

Athanasius Y. Samuel

Archbishop Athanasius Yeshue Samuel

Figure 39. Church letterhead cont. (February 6, 1953)

SYRIAN   PATRIARCHATE
OF ANTIOCH AND ALL THE EAST
DAMASCUS - SYRIA
U . A . R .

No. 302   ــهرﻠﻴﺎﻥ   26 th Oct, 1960

Ignatius   Jacob   III

Patriarch of Antioch and All the East

Apostolic Benediction to our spiritual children the church committee and parishioners
of St. Mary's Apostolic church of Worcester Mass ,

We gladly received your telegram , requesting us to open your church with
the name remaining St. Marye " Assyrian " Apostolic as we have promised you , and
awaiting our immediate instructions . It is true that we have already promised not
to change the name of your church . Now also we say that your church's name should
remain as it is . With regard to the opening of your church , you should approach
H. Eminence the Archbishop Mar Athanasius Y . Samuel as the church of West New York
did .

We hope that every thing will go smoothly .

May the Grace of our Lord be with you

Figure 40. Letterhead of the church, after the name change. (Oct. 26, 1960)

Only the Assyrian Church of the Virgin Mary in Paramus, New Jersey (made up of Assyrians from Omid/Diarbekir, Turkey) and Saint Mary's Assyrian Church in Worcester, Massachusetts (comprised of Kharput Assyrians) , retained their original Assyrian appellation. The conclusion of this is that the Assyrians of Kharput and Diarbekir obviously believed quite strongly in their Assyrian name, unlike many others who were more passive and accepting of the Church's change to "Syrian".

During the years following, many members of the "Jacobite" Church left and became members of the Church of the East. When asked why they left the Church even though two still retained the Assyrian name, one Roumel Kazar replied,

> *"Whom do these people take their orders from? They have no honor. The church took away our Assyrian identity, what is left?"*

Figure 41. The Kazar Family in Anatolia circa 1907.

The name change proved to be the beginning of the division within the Church of Antioch ("Jacobite") over the issue of Assyrianism. Many Kharputl Assyrians remained in the church hoping to continue the tradition despite the overall name change. Families were split, and quite often, heated words were exchanged upon occasions that brought them together.

The problems that persisted were immense. Slowly the entire

American Archdiocese under Bishop Yeshu Samuel began to decline to the present day where there is little if any cultural, humanitarian, or intellectual activity since the removal of the name.

The adoption of the anti-Assyrian dogma by the new "Syrian Orthodox Church", and the promotion of Arabism continue to hold sway to the modern day. Given that the Patriarchal See is presently in Damascus, it is probable that the Church is under political influence. Unfortunately the "Jacobite" Assyrians in the United States lack the religious authority to dispose of such erroneous mistakes, and indeed may be threatened by the clerical order.

In 1998 the Bishop Cyril Aphrem Karem of the East Coast of the United States took it upon himself to hold a meeting and underhandedly change the name of Saint Mary's Assyrian Orthodox Church to "Syrian". Though the matter had been in court for a time, the children of the Kharput Assyrians had less zeal than their parents had, and the newcomers of the church from other cities and villages also adopted an anti-Assyrian, pro-Arab, Turk, and Kurdish stance. Many a Kharput Assyrian who had passed away in recent years left this life in a shallow, sorrowful state, quite depressed at their easily influenced brethren.

Note: The terms "Syria" and "Syrian" though taken from Assyrian, have come today to mean people of the Arab Republic of Syria; and while many Assyrians were born in Syria, they are neither Arab nor Muslim and therefore calling them "Syrian" with the modern definition is erroneous. All Assyrians are the direct descendents, in an unbroken continuity from ancient days, of their forefathers. This problem finds its roots in the Hellenization of the Near East as stated in the introduction.

Social Institutions

In order to retain and promote Assyrian culture and heritage, the early settlers from Kharput began opening associations. The only threat to the Assyrians in the United States was assimilation into American culture; thus, these organizations were begun with the intent of continually reinvigorating Assyrianism among the Kharput people in New England. This process was slightly simpler than putting together a church because the meetings were held in houses, parks, and privately rented halls. Dr. Abraham K. Yousef started the earliest of these organizations in 1897 called the Assyrian Benevolent Association, before he left to Europe for educational purposes. The association met in both high and low times. He was also part of the Assyrian Five Association, which incorporated Assyrians from other villages, not only Kharput. Interestingly, the Assyrian Ladies Association of the church was started in 1908, almost 20 years before the church was even built. One must realize that at the time it was opened, there were relatively few Assyrians in the New England area.

Of course, from there, associations began popping up all around the area of Massachusetts spreading into Rhode Island where some Kharput Assyrians had settled. The most obvious reason for this is the fact that transportation was limited in the first half of the 20th century, and new immigrants to the United States rarely had enough money to afford the constant traveling to and from meetings.

Therefore in 1912, the Kharput Assyrians of the Boston area launched the Assyrian Young Men's Association of Boston. Though there were no more than a dozen Assyrians in the city of Lowell, Massachusetts, none-the-less, the Assyrian Mar Afram Benevolent Society of Lowell was established. In order to promote the education and intellectual pursuit of young Assyrians the Harpoot Assyrian United Educational Fund was born. Some got together in the Boston area under the umbrella of the Nineveh Association of Greater Boston. As stated earlier, some Kharput Assyrians settled in Rhode Island and founded the Assyrian St. Ephram Association of Central Falls, Rhode Island along with Assyrians from other villages in Turkey.

The Assyrians of Massachusetts were known for their hard work and dedication. But let us not leave out the Kharput Assyrians who settled in California. Seemingly another world away, some Assyrians found themselves working the alfalfa farms in Fresno, or the factories in Los Angeles. In comparison to those of New England, their impact on Assyrianism was minimal, although they retained close ties with their east coast brethren.

Figure 42. The Assyrian Benevolent Association of Worcester, MA. Est.1897 (A.K. Yousef standing 7th in from right) picture taken 1914.

Figure 43. Assyrian Five pamphlet 1919. In Assyrian and Armenian script.

Figure 44. Assyrian Ladies Association of Worcester, MA. Photo was taken in 1918 during the 10th year anniversary.

Figure 45. Assyrian Young Men's Association of Boston 1912.

Figure 46. Seal of the Assyrian Young Men's Association of Boston.

Figure 47. The Assyrian Young Adults Association of Boston, MA. Note the use of the silent A in the Syriac title of (As)syrian.

In the early 1940s, four organizations came together to solidify unity among Assyrians by creating a single organization. After numerous meetings in December of 1944, a unanimous vote permitted that a new organization be founded from among the previous four in the state of Massachusetts. On January 28th, 1945, the committee drafted the Constitution-By-Laws of the new association, which was comprised of the Assyrian Boston United Association, Harpoot United Association, Assyrian National Union and the Assyrian American Progressive Union. The United Assyrian Association of Massachusetts was incorporated on June 9' 1949. The bylaws were made and the objective stated as follows:

> "The object of this organization shall be to enliven the Assyrian spirit and to promote the intellectual, moral, and civic welfare of the Assyrian people."

The United Assyrian Association was instrumental in the purchase of land used for Assyrian picnics, and was later named Camp Nineveh. Unfortunately, the United States government, under the justification of "eminent domain" confiscated the land some years later. Thankfully though, many Assyrians were able to make use of the land before the seizure took place.

Assyrians from the city of Qamishly, Syria began to arrive in Worcester, Massachusetts in the 1960s and 1970s. They merged very well with the community that was already established, and with other Assyrian newcomers from Midyat, Turkey. Since most were college students, they wanted an association of their own without the interference of the adults. Thus they created the Assyrian Young Adults club which lasted for many years, until it was renamed the Beth Nahreen Assyrian Organization. In truth, these organizations were a major boon to the community in New England and helped incorporate new comers into the society.

In the case of the Assyrians of Kharput that arrived in the United States, many had begun producing literature and works that would promote their Assyrian heritage and strengthen the community, and some were known for their activism. One such person was the famous Dr. A. K. Yousef of Kharput.

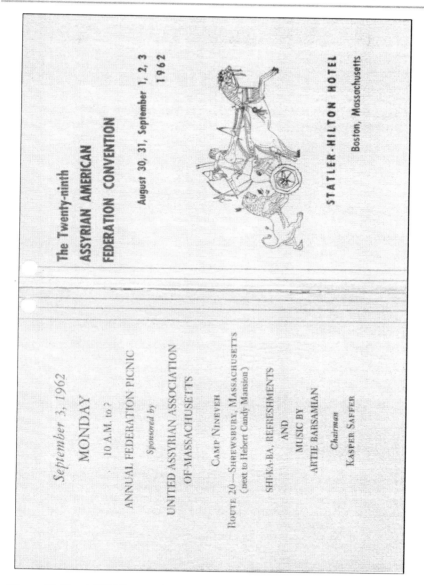

Figure 48. The AANF Convention in 1962 in Boston, MA sponsored by the United Assyrian Association of Massachusetts.

A Merry Christmas and a Happy New Year

United Assyrian Association of Massachusetts, Inc.

New Year's Eve
PARTY & FROLIC

Monday, December 31, 1951

AT THE BAIKAR HALL

296½ Shawmut Avenue (corner of Waltham Street)
BOSTON, MASSACHUSETTS

AMERICAN AND ORIENTAL MUSIC

David Safer, George Ohan and Co.

NOISE MAKERS   -   FAVORS   -   FOOD and REFRESHMENTS

Admission $1.00   Doors open 8:00 p. m.

COME AND HAVE FUN!

Figure 49. UAAM, Inc. New Years Eve party flyer. (1951)

Chapter 5: Famous Kharput Assyrians

Dr. Abraham K Yousef (1866 - 1924)

Figure 50. Portrait of Abraham K. Yousef.

Dr. Abraham K. Yousef was born in Kharput December 17, 1866. Growing up, he attended the Christian Mission School in Kharput and graduated from Central Turkey College in Aintab with a B.A. in 1886. He worked at the college as an instructor up until his departure in 1889 for the United States.[74] In 1895 he graduated from Baltimore Medical College with high honors and started his practice in Worcester, Massachusetts. Before leaving to Europe, he organized the Assyrian Benevolent Association in 1897.

In 1912 Dr. Yousef studied post-graduate courses in London and Vienna. Upon completion of courses dealing with diseases of the eyes, ears and throat, he left for Constantinople. He arrived at the onset of the Balkan Wars where he volunteered as a surgeon in the armed forces and for the Red Crescent Society. For his exceptional work he was given high praise and decorations from the Sultan during the cholera epidemic.[75]

Figure 51. Dr. Yousef during his work for the Red Cresent Society.

After returning to the United States, Captain Yousef would once again

---

[74] Assyria Online, www.aina.org/aol/Yoosuf.html

[75] Harold Perch, "Biography of Abraham K. Yousef" *Fiftieth Anniversary of St. Mary's Assyrian Apostolic Church*, (1974)

see the horrors of battle when America entered World War 1. He served well and attained the rank of Major. Upon seeing the devastation caused by the Turks, Kurds, Persians and Arabs towards his Assyrian people, he spent two years in Paris working on the Assyrian Cause during the Paris Peace Conference with fellow Assyrians Joel Warda, Yusuf Malek and others.

Returning frustrated, the destiny of the Assyrian people still not tangible, Captain Yousef would continue his work, helping to establish Saint Mary's Assyrian Apostolic Church of Worcester, Massachusetts in 1923. He was in fact the first president of the newly built church (in memory of the Church of the Virgin Mary in Kharput).

Captain Dr. Abraham K. Yousef was an extraordinary man. He wrote widely in *The Assyrian Progress, Beth Nahreen* and *The New Assyria* magazines. One of Dr. Yousef's best pieces was entitled "Assyria and the Peace Conference" in which he spoke on the Assyrians of Turkey, and more recently, the Assyrians in Iraq and the current problem they faced without a country at the end of the war.[76] He was a member of the American Medical Society, the Massachusetts State Society, and a founding member of the *Assyrian Five*, and *Assyrian Benevolent Association.*[77]

---

[76] Dr. A. K. Yousef, "The New Assyria" (Jan 15, 1919 volume 3 #29), 2.

[77] Harold Perch, "Biography of Abraham K. Yoosuf" *Fiftieth Anniversary of St. Mary's Assyrian Apostolic Church*, (1974).

Figure 52. Captain Abraham Yousef during the July 4th Parade in Worcester, MA, 1922.

Figure 53. Captain Dr. Abraham Yousef with his sister and her children.

Captain Yousef never married and thus took great interest in his nieces and nephews. A stalwart hero, he spent much of his time fighting for Assyrian rights in the United States and abroad. Although he found himself close to his sister's family, he was unable to watch the children grow as he past on at the young age of 58. He gave without any thought of reward, and helped others without concern for his own well-being. In the tradition of Professor Ashur Yousouf, Dr. Abraham exemplified the splendor of Assyrian generosity, honor and perseverance. He died in Worcester, Massachusetts December 26th, 1924.

There were many Assyrians of Kharput who would follow in the footsteps of Dr. A. K. Yousef. Some were his contemporaries, and others children of his contemporaries. Among them was one David Barsum Perley (Keshish).

Figure 54. Delegates to the League of Nations conference in Paris following World War I from the Assyrian people: Standing left to right – Said Radji, Moussa Shukur, *Hassio* Afrem Barsoom, Pierre Pacus, Brother Aram Ablahad. Sitting left to right – Captain A.K. Yousef, Rustem Najib, Dr. Jean Zabony, Rev. Yoel E. Warda, Said Anthony Namik.

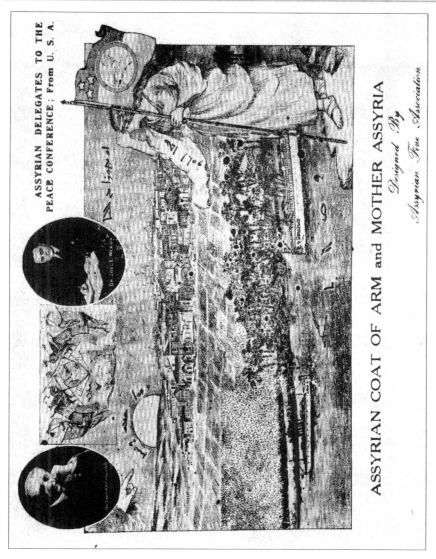

Figure 55. Card designed by the Assyrian Five Association. Includes photos of Dr. Yousef (left) and Youel Warda (right)

David B. Perley (Keshish) J.S.D. (1901 –1979)

Figure 56. Picture of David Perley in 1930 as seen in Yusuf Malek's, The British Betrayel of the Assyrians.

David Barsum Keshish was born in 1901 in Kharput, Turkey to Barsam and Vatar Keshish. As one of six children he lived his early childhood in the village. After some time, young David would graduate from the American Apostolic School of Kharput in 1918. In 1922 he escaped the massacres where his father died a martyr at the hands of the Ottoman Turkish regime.

His trials and tribulations with his cousin Djordjis (George) during the Assyrian Genocide in 1914-1918 are recounted in the Appendix. In fact they traveled through the Dersin Mountains in Russia and further east before leaving to the United States two years later.

In 1926 he received a B.A. from Boston University's College of Liberal Arts. Soon after he went to law school and received an M.A. from Boston University's School of Law in 1928. At New York University he continued studying law and received his Ph.D. in 1933.[78]

In 1933 the Assyrians around the world fell in shock as word spread of the massacre in the Assyrian village of Simele in Northern Iraq (Assyria) by the Iraqi regime. After this horrendous event, Assyrians in the United States realized steps had to be taken in order to prevent an atrocity like Simele from occurring again. They founded the Assyrian American National Federation in 1933 to protect Assyrian rights and heritage. Dr. Perley worked as President of the Federation from June 1934 through October 1935 where upon he took over as vice-president for a time.

In 1935 Yusuf Malek wrote the famous The British Betrayal of the Assyrians from an eyewitness perspective. He then requested his good friend David Perley to write one segment on the "Jacobite" Assyrians knowing that the majority of the book centered around the Assyrians in Iraq, mainly the "Chaldean" and "Nestorian." Upon completing the chapter on "The Jacobites", Perley stated his feelings about being a "Jacobite" Assyrian thus:

> *Jacobites are Jacobites only by virtue of their religious faith; they are Assyrians by virtue of their nationality. As such they resent any injustice that is directed against any part of their national composition, for –*
>
> *"No distance breaks the tie of blood; Brothers are brothers evermore."*[79]

---

[78] ܩܘܝܐ ܐܝܪܟܐ ܐܘܒܬ܂ ܐܬܘܪܝܐ ܐܬܘܪܝܐ ܐܬܠܬܚܕ. (Tehran, Iran: Assyrian Youth Cultural Society Press, 1970), 339-340.

[79] Yusuf Malek, The British Betrayal of the Assyrians, "The Jacobites" by David Barsum Perley J.S.D. (Chicago: The Assyrian National Federation & The Assyrian National League of America, 1935), 127.

Dr. Perley married Miss Rose Kazanchy of Paterson, New Jersey where he established his office and raised his young daughter Penna. Perley would write both within the Assyrian and American circles. He was quite often besieged with letters praising his work on behalf of his people. Many even wondered how he made time for his law practice. Between writing books, articles in "ܟܘܟܒܐ ܕܐܬܘܪ" (The Assyrian Star Magazine) and other periodicals both Assyrian and American, David Perley was a man of tireless action.

Perley was the epitome of the Assyrian intellectual. Not long after helping out with Malik's book, he wrote <u>Whither Christian Missions?</u> in 1944. The book centered on the Church of the East and the Assyrian question in Iraq after the Massacre of Simele. Dr. Perley and other Assyrian intellectuals in the United States felt compelled to speak out against the atrocities still being committed against the Assyrians in the Middle East. Perley first wrote the book as a reaction to the despicable comments of one missionary by the name John Van Ess of the Foreign Missions of the Reformed Church in America, against the Assyrian people. John Van Ess had sided with the government of Iraq and showed friendly splendor towards it in the wake of one of the worst acts of ethnic cleansing ever precipitated by a governmental body.[80]

David Perley would continue along the path of Assyrianism throughout his life. On June 6th, 1947 he participated in "The Middle East In The Post War World National And Religious Minorities" discussion at New York University - School of Education. There he gave an introductory speech on "The Assyrians", their history and present situation. Though he had many supporters and academics with which he conversed, among those the great William B. Ziff author of <u>The Rape of Palestine</u>, there were those who had no sympathy for the Assyrians, or their dire situation. To such regrettable people and their attempt to "sweep the Assyrian plight under the rug" Perley had this to say:

> "The soul of Assyrian is spiritual through and through and not material. You can not destroy that which is spiritual; it is coexistent with eternity."[81]

In response to a Wall Street Journal article written by Dr. Leo Oppenheim of Chicago questioning the genealogy of the Assyrians, David Perley challenged

---

[80] David Barsum Perley, J.S.D., <u>Whither Christian Missions?</u> Revised Edition, (NJ: Kimball Press, 1946), 2-3.

[81] Yusuf Malek, <u>The British Betrayal of the Assyrians</u>, "The Jacobites" by David Barsum Perley J.S.D. (Chicago: The Assyrian National Federation & The Assyrian National League of America, 1935), 114-115.

Oppenheim to a public debate, and until such time as he agreed, Perley demanded he no longer publish such statements on Assyrians. Perley also, on numerous occasions, defended the ancient Assyrians specifically when he replied to the historian Arnold Toynbee, amongst others, who spoke on the Assyrians as the "inventors of cruelty".

David Barsum Perley, J.S.D., died in 1979 leaving behind a legacy for young Assyrian children to follow. Many individuals found David's path of Assyrianism one of true life and passion. Francis Emmanuel Hoyen, Jr. was one of those individuals.

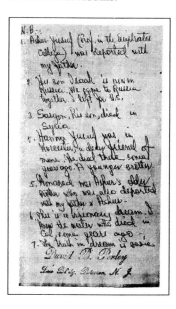

1) Ashur Yusuf (Prof. In the Euphrates College) was deported with my father.
2) His son Isaak is now in Russia. We came to Russia together. I left for US.
3) Sargon, his son, died in Syria.
4) Hanna Yusuf was in Worcester, a dear friend of mine. He died there some years ago. A younger brother.
5) Donabed was Ashur's older brother who was also deported with my father and Ashur.
6) There is a visionary dream. I knew the waiter who died in Cal. some years ago.
7) The truth in dream is basic.
David B. Perley

Figure 57. Some notes in the handwriting of David Perley.

Francis Emmanuel Hoyen, Jr.

Francis was truly man of vision and action. The son of Francis E. and Elizabeth (Donabed) Hoyen was born in Worcester, Massachusetts in the late 1920s. Although knowing little of The Great Depression when he was a child, his parents worked hard to provide him with a good life. He received his Bachelors of Education in 1950 from Worcester State College.

In 1954, Francis Emmanuel wrote a book entitled, Was Jesus Really Born in Beth-Lehem?, where he argued at the Assyrian bloodlines of Jesus Christ. Hoyen explains the way the Assyrians used to supplant their own people into conquered territories to make rebellion less likely. Samaria and Galilee were two cities were this was done. Of course, Jesus is many times referred to as the "Galilean"; and historians tell how the Israelis and the Judeans looked down upon the Samaritans and Galileans. In fact, Hoyen makes reference to the etymology of Galilee, which comes from the root *galutha*, which means captivity or exile, outside of original home (a negative connotation usually).[82] He also stresses the importance of the problem with the Magi from the East. St. Ephraim believed that they were Assyrians who came to pay homage to the Christ, a point that he also speaks about. Indeed, Hoyen makes solid arguments in his work, many of which will probably be studied in the future.

This was not just the passion of an individual, but it seems to have run in the family. F. Emmanuel Hoyen Sr. composed a poem for Assyrians in the aftermath of *Shato Du Sayfo.*[83]

Assyrian Song
Oh! Sons of Asshur arise and do your share,
The glorious hours are nigh, we must now be there;
Worthy of such ties, we must now conquer and guide
The enemies' leaders and ambitious pride.
Chorus
Joined in arms, boys, ahead we must go,
And clean our world of such scandalous foes;
By doing it now a good lesson we will give,
Which they will never forget as long as they live.

---

[82]Francis Emmanuel Hoyen, Jr., Was Jesus Really Born in Beth-Lehem?, (May 1954), 88.

[83] "Year of the Sword"– Refers to the years of 1914-1918 in which the Assyrians lost 2/3rds of their entire population.

Let us break the chains, and break them today,
And free our country and open the way
To see our historical Nineveh as it was before,
And all its beautiful surroundings that we so adore.
Onward let us go until we get to Assyria, for joy and happiness will follow our
Victoria;
We will have some tough fighting, but will not mind,
To destroy our enemy for mankind.
By Son of Ashur,
Francis E Hoyen[84]

Seemingly militaristic, this poem was composed when Assyrians had been fleeing their homeland in the greatest mass exodus of its time. They were frustrated, had been betrayed by the western powers, and they were desperate for a place to call home. Thus, Assyrianism grew even more in the hearts of the people who shared a common hardship, a common enemy, and a common longing.

In 1922, before Francis Emmanuel's time, a young Nimrud Asshur Hoyen composed a hymn for the "Jacobite" Assyrians that centered on pride in both Church and Nation. Thus many were given a sneak peak into the later work of Francis Hoyen.

Francis worked for many years as a clerk in the Assessors' department, and tirelessly for many years promoting the cause of the Assyrians in the United States, and specifically in Worcester. As a substitute teacher in the Worcester Public Schools, he was known for his intellect and vitality. He cared a great deal for the teaching profession, that he went back to Worcester State College and received his Masters Degree in Counseling in 1977. He was a Deacon of Saint Mary's Assyrian Apostolic Church through the stages of his life. Indeed, it was said of those who knew Francis, he was very dispirited at the end of his life over the changing of the name of the Church from Assyrian to "Syrian".

Unfortunately, he died at his home on March 24, 1999 at the age of 69. His friends remain steadfast with the claim that there was never a gentler man, never one so caring. I also knew him, and say he was all the praise, and much more. He will never be forgotten in the Assyrian community, and by all of those whose lives he touched.

---

[84] The New Assyria June 15, 1919 vol 3 # 34 (New Assyria Publishing Company Jersey City NJ), 10.

Figure 58. The <u>Assyrian Patriotic Song</u> written by Nimrod Asshur Hoyen in 1924. Interestingly this song was heavily focused towards the "Jacobite" sect.

Figure 59. cont.

Figure 60. cont.

Aphrem George Hoyen (1906-1970)

Aphrem George Hoyen was born August 5, 1906 in Lowell, Massachusetts to George (July 20, 1878) and Natalie (August 20, 1884) both of Kharput. With brother Sargon (June 15, 1912) also born in Lowell, the family moved to Worcester, Massachusetts in 1922. His musical career began at St. Ann's Episcopal Church in Lowell, Massachusetts. He was a graduate of South High School and the New England Conservatory of Music in Boston, where he obtained his bachelor of music degree in 1931.

Soon after completing his studies in Boston, he went to Europe on a scholarship, and was the first to receive a diploma and certificate of honor at the International Stiftung Mozateum in Salzburg, Austria. He then made his debut as conductor of the famed Salzburg Festival, and later conducted the Stadorkestern in Finland.

"George" as he was most often called, proved quite a proficient conductor and later found himself conducting tours of South America including Chile, Colombia, Peru, and Panama among other countries. The Assyrian American National Federation honored him for his outstanding accomplishments as an Assyrian Musician. When he moved to California, George formed the World Symphony Orchestra. As a man of both vision and principle, he hoped strongly for cultural respect and awareness through world music. He died on May 27, 1970 in West Los Angeles, California.

Fawlos Gabriel

Figure 65. Fawlos Gabriel of Kharput. Teacher of *Taw Meem Simkath* School in Lebanon.

Fawlos Gabriel was another proponent in the Assyrian cause. A child of the massacres, he was raised in the Assyrian Orphanage of Adana. After the deportations from Kharput, many Assyrians found themselves in Lebanon, attempting to reconcile their lives and future plans. *Malphono* Fawlos Gabriel, along with others, saw a vision of an Assyrian school for children (especially orphans) that would aid the revival of their culture while remaining somewhat far from their original homeland. Fawlos Gabriel became one of the founding members of the Assyrian school Taw Meem Simkath. He was a teacher of Assyrian at the Lebanese University School of Arts. Fawlos Gabriel also aided in the assembly of a three-volume book of learning Assyrian. Although he spent years away from his homeland as well, he, like many other, found comfort in poetry and song, as a way in which to express his longing and passionate feelings for his people and heritage.

Figure 61. Assyrian Orphanage School (*Taw Meem Simkath*) 1924, Beyrouth.

Farid Nuzha (January 10, 1894 - 1971)

The tale of Farid Nuzha is a less known story. He was born in Hamah, Syria on January 10, 1894. Farid's grandfather *Mardu* left Kharput in 1760 to settle in Hamah. Farid was educated in the Assyrian style by the clergy of the "Jacobite" Church through elementary school. Although one of the top students, Nuzha left to be home-schooled after a dispute arose between the clergy and his father.

In June of 1911, seventeen Assyrian families left the "Jacobite" Church and became members of the Catholic Church in Hamah. Due to this issue, Farid's father fought with his cousins who had become powerful leaders in the Catholic Church. He protested that those Assyrians who leave the "Jacobite" or "Nestorian" Churches would eventually lose their culture. So adamant was he, that he pushed young *Malphono* Nuzha to travel to South America in order to find freedom to speak his mind, and educate himself free from political and religious restraints.

The following month, *Malphono* Farid Nuzha left for Argentina where he would study business and mathematics. In 1920 he met an Italian woman whom he fell enamored with, married, and left to Italy for a time. After eleven years, Farid returned to Argentina to establish himself and continue his previous Assyrian nationalistic work. He helped start the Assyrian Good Will Organization for which he was a writer in newsletters and periodicals. On August 1, 1934 he founded *St. Afrem* the Assyrian Organization in Buenos Aires.

Highly influenced by Naum Faik and his *Beth Nahrain* newspaper, he published *Asiria* magazine from 1943 to 1959 in Assyrian, Spanish, and Arabic. The magazine would cover various topics from social, cultural, and humanitarian aid issues. Nuzha was a strong proponent of publicizing the Assyrian Genocide and various genocides through which the Assyrians had been subjected to in the past.

Nuzha was perhaps the single greatest proponent of an Assyrian homeland during the first half of the 20th Century. He was instrumental in gaining support for the establishment of a sovereign Assyrian nation in Brazil. Despite being a temporary solution to the settlement of his people, Nuzha was aided and granted permission by various governments to begin the arrangement. Yet, later tension between the Lady Surma Khanim of the Church of the East, and various Assyrian national leaders, the goal never materialized. Farid Nuzha died in 1971 never seeing his homeland again.

112

Professor Ashur Yousouf (1858 - 1915)

Figure 62. Professor Ashur Yousouf

There is not very much known of Ashur Yousouf's early life and writings since much of it was destroyed by the Turkish military insurrections in 1915. Ashur Yousouf was born in Kharput in 1858. Dr. Yousouf received his formal education at Central Turkey College and taught throughout the area from Kharput, Amasia and Smyrna, all the way to Antioch.[85] Professor Yousouf was awarded a degree from the Turkish Bureau of Education. He was the editor of the Assyrian monthly magazine, *Murshid D'Athur* that was in publication for six years until the time of his death.[86] He was a professor at Euphrates College,

---

[85] Yusuf Malek, The British Betrayal of the Assyrians, "The Jacobites" by David Barsum Perley J.S.D. (Chicago: The Assyrian National Federation & The Assyrian National League of America, 1935), 115.

[86] "The Assyrian National Directory in the US for 1960", Assyrian National Federation, Kimball Press, (NJ: 1960)

which was located within the *willayet* of Kharput. He had a brother Donabed, a wife and two sons named Sargon and Isaak. The tragic last days of Ashur Yousouf's life are best told by him, for only he could describe so eloquently how his life ended, and his final thoughts before he died[87]:

> *Monday April 20, 1915*
> *From my cell to my beloved brother,*
> *Hanna Yousouf in America.*
>
> *Yesterday on Sunday morning April 19th 1915 when we had heard that the Turks were crazed with the anger of beastly slaughter, sparing neither man woman or child (unless she was fair to lustful eyes) we became terrified. Especially when the news came of the arrests of my comrades, I began to shiver, and during the course of preparing a hiding place, I myself was arrested and brought to this cell.*
>
> *This is a good opportunity that I am enjoying to write you my last letter, for I know we will be cut to pieces when we leave here, though I do not know when and where.*
>
> *Do not worry over my death-it is God's will- I am going to heaven to protect the rights of the Assyrians at the presence of the biggest and greatest Judge. The books and the work I had started about our nation's education remain unfinished. I am afraid they will be destroyed in a very short time. One of my biggest desires has been to keep our brother Donabed away from drink. I'd have given anything under the sun to have made him temperate but it was in vain. I will give him my last advice after I finish writing to you.*
>
> *I leave my loving wife and children in your care. My son Isaak was to graduate from high school this year. I had intended to give him a college education, which is another unfinished task I leave in your hands.*
>
> *The time is almost up and I close this sad missile with wishes for your welfare and safety, so that God may some day lead you to revenge on your enemies!*
>
> *Farewell brother, farewell!*
> *Ashur S. Yousouf*

Yousouf and others were taken to the "red prison" where they awaited death. While in prison they were tortured mercilessly. In Document 69 of Lord Bryce's Treatment of the Armenians in the Ottoman Empire it was stated that the hair of his head (Professor Ashur Yousouf), moustache and beard were pulled out in an attempt to pin a confession of treason against him. He was then starved and hung by his arms for a day and a night, beaten, had his fingernails extracted, his eyes gouged out, and physically stigmatized by the merciless Turks with scalding metal pokers. Thus Assyrians lost many men and women of power and intellect.

---

[87] George Sefer, Dream of a Long Journey
www.bethsuryoyo.com/images/articles/ashuryousif/ardocs27.htm

Unfortunately Ashur Yousouf's son Sargon also died but in Syria; when and how is uncertain. Some of his family managed to escape to "Armenia" and have remained there since the massacres. His son Isaak apparently went to Russia for a time before finally making it to Massachusetts in the United States. Ashur Yousouf of Kharput, Assyrian Nationalist, writer, poet, professor, husband and father, along with Donabed his older brother, Barsum Keshish and about 2000 other Assyrians and Armenians died together on April 21, 1915; martyred at the hands of the Ottomans. Thus we enter the major exodus of the Assyrians from Kharput.

NOTE: Although little if anything is ever mentioned about the Assyrian Holocaust by Armenian and Western writers, I have chosen to add the Armenians in this paper as in many cases Assyrians were killed alongside Armenians in the wake of the war and to speak of one and not the other would not only be improbable, it would also be abhorrent. Also, the reader must be given the knowledge that <u>2/3 of the total Assyrian population (including all churches and sects) was wiped off the face of the earth between 1915-1918 and *never* acknowledged</u>.

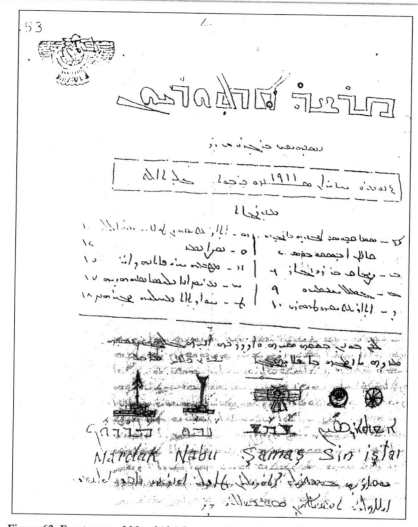

Figure 63. Front page of *Murshid Athuryoon* (Assyrian Guide), published by Ashur Yousouf in Kharput in 1911 .

Figure 64. Another segment of *Murshid Athuryoon.* Poem at the bottom translated as, "Harput, When I hear your name I hurt. From top to bottom I shiver. Let us tell each other our sorrows, for I am from that place as well."

Photos of Kharput Assyrians of in New England

Figure 65. Young men of Kharput. Top Youhana and Elias Donabed. Far left, Sam Samuel. (Others unknown)

Figure 66. George Alexander (US 1942). A young Kharput Assyrian.

Figure 67. The Assyrians at a party in Worcester, MA enjoying the company of friends and the delight of their native music. (Circa 1950)

Figure 68. "Three close friends." Youhana Donabed, George Donabed, and David Safer.

Figure 69. Wedding picture of Sargon Arslan and Shmuni Samuel
(Massachusetts Circa 1940).

Figure 70. Mr and Mrs. David Safer on their wedding day (Circa 1940).

Figure 71. Another Safer Family of Kharput. Many Assyrians also carried this surname. From top, left to right: Abdenur, David, and their brother and sister.　(Circa 1930)

Figure 72. Family. Left to right: Bishara, Sidon, Elias, Miriam and Behnam Donabed.
(Boston, MA Circa 1935)

.

Figure 73. A Kharput Assyrian, J. Deinha in uniform (Circa 1945). There were many popular Assyrian names, which were used by the larger families of Kharput. Deinha, Donabed, Safer, Dasho, Perch, Yousef, Sahag, Bedig, Barsum, and Qazar among others.

Figure 74. Bishara Donabed in military attire. (Sept 20, 1942)

Figure 75. The Donabeds at work in George's Tayloring Shop. (Circa 1945)

There were many other prominent Kharput Assyrian-Americans, (John Dasho, artist, Ashur Chavoor, Assyrian-activist, etc.) yet to tell each of their stories would take a lifetime. Those people specified here will give the reader an idea of how important the Assyrian identity was to them, and how hard they worked to keep their dreams alive. I would only add one more thing to this: the above people whom I have mentioned, and indeed countless others, were not only great Assyrians, they were also phenomenal people. They lived the lives of the righteous:

"To laugh often and much, to win the respect of intelligent people and the affection of children, to earn the appreciation of honest critics and endure the betrayal of false friends, to appreciate beauty, to find the best in others, to leave the world a bit better, whether by a healthy child, a garden patch...to know even one life has breathed easier because you have lived. This is to have succeeded!"

— Ralph Waldo Emerson

Chapter 6: The Recent Years

Figure 76. The plain of Elazig. A view of the city taken in the summer of 2003 from the mountain top. As of today, approximately 4 Assyrian families remain in Elazig. Those who remain are not necessarily original Kharput Assyrians. Most are forced to take Turkish surnames and have since become quite culturally Turkish.

The Kharput community today has since withered. Most Assyrians have passed on, and those that are still alive remember little of the old village. The church on Hawley Street was sold and a new church opened on Route 9 in Shrewsbury, MA. Unfortunately since the changing of the name from Assyrian to "Syrian", the descendants of Kharput Assyrians have boycotted, seeking solace within other churches rather than the mother church that had betrayed them.

The United Assyrian Association of Massachusetts, Inc. has become a shell of an organization. For the past fifteen years there has been almost nothing in production from an organization, which was once held in such high esteem. The members, for many years, were no longer Kharput Assyrians, and cared little for the well being of the Assyrian people. Until recently, the organization had become stagnant. In recent years some active Assyrians have returned and now fund student scholarships and aid Assyrian humanitarian organizations such as the Assyrian Aid Society headed by the world-renowned Assyrian chef, Narsai David.

Some former members of the Assyrian Young Adults Club have gone from generating *Had B Nison* (Assyrian New Year) parties, to funding Assyrian lectures at Harvard University, Columbia University, Georgetown University and others. With the help of the David B. Perley Assyrian Book Fund at Harvard, these Assyrians of Massachusetts (with various Kharput remnants among them) have been a beacon of hope for a community struggling to keep alive memories of accomplishments and achievements.

The David Barsam Perley Assyrian Book Fund at Harvard has helped Drs. Eden Naby and Michael Hopper in collecting the most impressive modern Assyrian history collection in the world today. The book fund, which was started by the Assyrians in memory of the great David Perley, has helped to accumulate a wealth of resources on the modern Assyrian communities in every aspect of their lives, from books and magazines to music and entertainment.

The memory of Ashur Yousouf, David Perley and other Kharput Assyrians live on today in such places as *Huyodo* (Union) magazine by the Assyrian society in Sweden. Also, the Assyrian Democratic Organization was founded on the ideals of Ashur Yousouf and Naum Faik, the Assyrian nationalist from Diarbekir (Omid). The famous Assyrian poet Ninos Aho, friend of the late David Perley, helps to keep alive the memories of these great Assyrians through his poetry. Thus, though these once distinguished Assyrians have passed on from this life, their vision has not been forgotten by the Assyrians of the 21st Century.

As for the village, there was little to remind people of the once thriving mountain home. The gravestones of the Assyrians had all been pillaged. All that remains are rocks and red earth to mark generations of Kharput Assyrians. The houses have all been destroyed, their wood stripped by the marauding brigands. Oddly, the remains of the fortress are still "thriving."

The church had been but a shell of its former glory. (All the icons and valuable artifacts that remained were moved to Saint George's Assyrian Church in Elazig, or stolen by invaders.) All that remained were the window in the wall, and the great stone imbedded into the church ground, upon which the ill were healed of their maladies.

Figure 77. Another angle of the Assyrian Church of St. Mary in 1980 during the Samuel family's visit.

Figure 78. The Assyrian Church of St. Mary, June 2003. The entrance on the lower right corner.

Figure 79. View from the north-east of the Church of St. Mary. (June 2003)

Figure 80. Archbishop Aktas of Tur Abdien at the service held at the Assyrian Church of the Virgin Mary in Kharput 2000. (photo courtesy of *Voice of Tur Abdin*)

Figure 81. Assyrians enjoying the traditional music played on the bass clarinet 2000. Archbishop Samuel Aktas and Fr. Yusuf Akbulut on hand. (Photo courtesy of *Voice of Tur Abdien*)

This has been the case for many years, but things have changed

133

recently. During the most recent solar eclipse, the mountain home saw tourists blanketing the countryside eager to see the eclipse that would pass directly over the old church of the Virgin Mary. Many scientists and sightseers built up part of the area in an attempt to record the wondrous cosmic event. Thus the village received its first taste of its rebuilt glory. Soon after this time, the church celebrated a mass for the first time in decades. Assyrians and onlookers lined the paths of Kharput to celebrate this historic event.

Some Assyrians have returned to Kharput. In recent years, there are only a handful of people there at the current time, but in the future their numbers may increase as economic and humanitarian conditions improve.

This realization may be difficult for some to understand for many western and eastern readers. Conditions in Turkey seem to be much better than other places in the Middle East. In truth, it may be quite worse in some ways. As in Diarbekir and Tur Abdien, the Assyrians are not allowed to teach their history, culture (including language) and religion. The government tolerates their religious beliefs, but in no way are they allowed the same freedoms as Muslims in the same area.

Many Kurmanjis live along the mountain paths where the Assyrians once made their homes. They retain their nomadic lifestyle and such, but have little respect for the Assyrian ancestry of the area. Indeed the government has done very little to protect the Assyrians and their heritage. Graffiti covers much of the old fortress, and indeed much of the Assyrian Church as well.

The Turkish government has maintained a policy of silent assimilation of the Assyrians. The first generation of Assyrians that immigrated from Kharput have since past on. Most of what remains are old pictures, worn and shabby, yet nevertheless still shining with character. Cemeteries contain some of the last intimates of these Assyrians.

Figure 82. The slightly renovated altar of the Assyrian Church. Since 2000, the church has seen mass on special occasions and holidays.

Figure 83. A few of the older buildings left in the vicinity of Kharput. Most havebeen destroyed or in the case of the odd building, renovated and turned into a restaurant. (June 2003)

Figure 84. Lower bathhouse. (June 2003)

Figure 85. The citidel overlooking the plains of Kharput and the Euphrates river in the background. (2003)

Figure 86. The fortress entrance in the summer of 2003. Lack of respect for indigeounous cultures continuous to be a problem throughout the world, especially in the Middle East.

Figure 87. Remains near the fortress. (June 2003)

Figure 88. Ruins of an Armenian Church. (June 2003)

Figure 89. The Assyrian Church of St. Mary, June 2003 with ruins in the foreground, part of the citidel on the far right, and the Euphrates river far off in the distance. The church is impossible to see from any attacking point, making its positioning pure genius.

Figure 90. The upper bathhouse. Bathhouses were quite important to the sanitation of the town. The intricate architecture is a testament to its value.

Figure 91. Entrance to the upper bathhouse. (2003)

Figure 92. A view of the Assyrian Quarter on the northside of the church. In the early 1900s, hundreds of houses filled the landscape. (2003)

Figure 93. A view from the Assyrian Quarter today, with the Euphrates off in the distance. (June 2003)

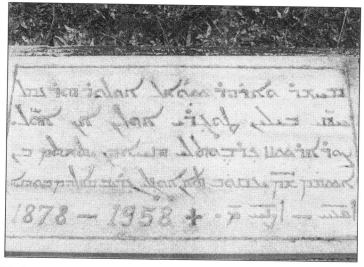

Figure 94. Gravestone of Jacob Tanoglu in Elazig. Written in Assyrian script and Turkish language.

Figure 95. The grave of *Shamosho* "Deacon" Yusuf Tanoglu. (2003)

Figure 96. Kharput Assyrian head stone in Watertown, MA. (2001)

Figure 97. Assyrian headstone in Watertown, MA. (2001)

Figure 98. Kharput grave of the Donabed family. (Watertown, MA. 2001)

Figure 99. Headstone with the serto or Assyrian "Jacobite" script. (Watertown, MA. 2001)

Figure 100. Assyrian gravestone of Youhanna and Roumel Donabed, and Abdonoor and Margaret Safer. (Milton, MA 2001)

Figure 101. Estrangele script Headstone of *Shamosho* Samuel Samuel and wife Sidon Behnam Donabed Samuel. Notice the two Assyrian stars of Shamash to either side of the eastern cross. At the bottom *Othuroye* "Assyrians". (Watertown, Massachusetts)

Gabriel Namen, 76; lawyer for 49 years

Gabriel A. Namen, 76, a Worcester lawyer 49 years, died Monday in City Hospital after being stricken in his home, 22 Audubon Road.

Mr. Namen practiced law at 332 Main St. and previously at 311 Main St.

He leaves his wife, Elizabeth B. (Gatti) Namen; a daughter, Brenda G.N., wife of Carl E. Hellstrom; his mother, Elmas (Elbag) Namen Yoosuf; a brother, Hanna A. Namen, all of Worcester; a half-sister, Anushig Janigian of East Providence, R.I.; a grandson, Jed A. Hellstrom of Worcester, and nieces and nephews.

Born in Harpoot, Assyria, he lived in Worcester 62 years. His father was the late Anthony Namen.

Mr. Namen attended Classical High School and graduated from High School of Commerce. He attended Clark University and graduated from Northeastern University School of Law in 1936.

He was a member of American Trial Lawyers Association, and Worcester County, Massachusetts and American Bar associations.

Mr. Namen was a director of Worcester Legal Aid Society, a trustee of the Bar Insurance Program, and served on various Worcester County Bar Association committees.

Gabriel A. Namen

ciating, assisted by the Rev. Shamoun Asmar and the Rev. David Miller.

Burial will at the convenience of the family.

There are no calling hours.

The family requests flowers be omitted.

Donations may be made instead to St. Mary's Assyrian Apostolic Church Memorial Fund, 17 Hawley

Figure 102. Obituary of Gabriel Namen of Kharput. Notice place of birth in the forth paragraph: *Harpoot, Assyria.*

Figure 103. The above picture is the headstone of the Kashish and Kasab families. The Assyrian symbol for the trinity resplendent at the top, and a quote of the great David Barsum Perley sits at the bottom. "The soul of Assyria is spiritual through and through, and that which is spiritual is coexistent with eternity."

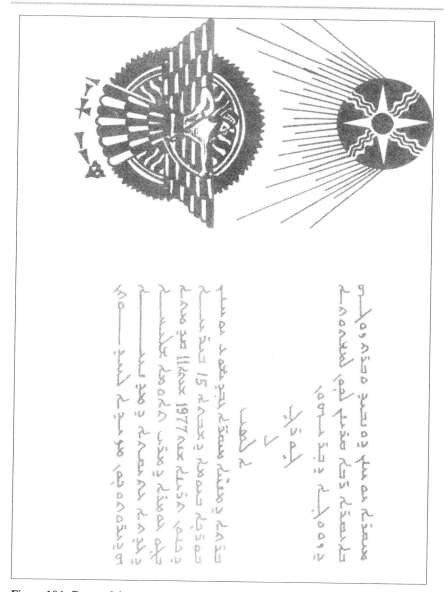

Figure 104. Cover of the wedding invitation of George Donabed (son of Youhana and Roumel Donabed of Kharput) to Elsie (daughter of Odisho and Jerusha Youkhana) in New Britain, Connecticut, January 15, 1977.

Conclusion

This book has been concerned with telling the story of the Assyrians of Kharput to the reader in a fashion that would help retain the memories of these people without changing their personalities. It is notable to comment on the character of the Kharput Assyrians by saying: These were a durable people who lived in hard times. They arrived in America because they were survivors of a war and a holocaust that is unnamed and non-existent to the modern world. Were it not for perseverance they would have all met death at the savage hands of the Turks and "Kurds" in 1915-1918.

They did their best to prevent the inevitable; for as with all communities that have come to the United States, assimilation is almost certain, especially by the third generation. Though the first generation Assyrians did their best to prevent the demise of their community, the lack of an immediate threat (as in Kharput) allowed for the easier integration of American social values, ideas, and habits. To most students of social history, this would be but another example of a community assimilating into American society without much in the way of continued ties to their heritage. I beg to differ. For two generations the Assyrians of Kharput thrived with their children despite not having an Assyrian language to act as a further link. The language both they and their children spoke were the languages of *nukhroye*[88]. So despite difficulties they managed to persevere in some areas.

The Assyrian American National Federation that is in existence today owes most of its continued success to the *Kharputoye* founders and builders of the organization. Even now, third generation Kharput Assyrians have begun tracing their roots, in search of their identity. Some of the children of Kharput Assyrians, like Mr. Kasper Safer, have put together oral historical documents in

---

[88] "Strangers/Outsiders/Enemies" from the Akkadian Assyrian *nukru* the k becoming *rkikhtha* or "spirantized".

order to keep the memory of his ancestors alive. Of course, as the knowledge is passed on, it survives.

The area of Assyrian Studies is quite vast, and has not been touched on often enough. Unfortunate misnomers about identity and language have caused problems for would-be scholars in the area of Assyrian Studies. Also, there is no shortage of material. In the Kharput plains alone there were approximately 300 villages (some may have only consisted of a family or two) and the Hakkari terrain was as large as modern day Lebanon. The expanse of geographical area that the Assyrians encompassed for the last 1000 years is quite vast. Thus, perhaps the future will allow for further inspection of all Assyrian territories, and a greater look into the history of Kharput. For theirs' was a community of honor, humility, and a spirit so vibrant it shook the pillars of tradition for generations to come.

Figure 105. Kharput Assyrians picnic photo 1929, Worcester, Massachusetts. left to right: top: George Ovaness, Kasper Safer, George Elbag, Herbert George, Kander ?, Elbi, ?, George Samuel, ?, Alfred George; middle: Charles Safer, Salim Elbi, Youhana Donabed, Mack Chavoor, Daniel Alexander, George Donabed (RI), Samuel Samuel, William Baptist, Jacob Chavoor, Simon Arslan, Art Arslan, George Hoyen; middle lower: Abdednur Safer, David Safer, Harold Perch, Charles Perch, Henry Perch, Abe Elbag, Peter Hoyen, :ground: George Kashish, Albert Perch, Bell Azerian, Yousef Papas, "Bagels" John Ohan, Jake Samuel (California), Emanuel Perch (son of Ziama), ?, William Perch, Peter Perch, Albert Perch.

Appendix

There is no better historian than the eyewitness to events. Thus we have the story of young George Tomas Kashish, cousin to Dr. David Barsam Perley of Kharput and nephew to martyr Barsam Perley. We have the following account from a book entitled Shall this Nation Die? by Rev. Joseph Naayem.

What Happened at Kharput

At the end of 1918 I met, at Constantinople, Djordjis Toumas Keshishe[89], a businessman of Kharput, who had been an eyewitness of the massacres, which took place in that town. I wrote down the following account, word for word, at his dictation, and, the better to authenticate the details of his narrative obtained his signature to my notes.

"The Turks commenced by arresting certain men of note, in particular the schoolmasters. Among others, they seized Oshous (Ashur) Yussef, Professor at the American College and editor of the "Murshed,"(Monitor of the Assyrian People) the Assyrian organ of the town. If I remember rightly, this was at the beginning of May 1915. Those arrested were imprisoned for a fortnight. Their houses were searched, but happily nothing of a compromising nature was discovered. The dwellings of the Assyrians or Jacobites were also subjected to the same measure.

Meanwhile, Sabit Bey, Governor of the town, betook himself to Erzerum, where, on a pretext that there was an epidemic of typhus, he closed all the schools. From Erzerum he returned as far as Mezre on a Friday some days later.

Taking up his quarters at the Seraglio he held a council, which lasted for over an hour, during which time Christians were forbidden to enter the building. I happened to be with friends in the courtyard of the church, where I had hidden to escape military service. While there I noticed armed soldiers making their rounds. Towards nine o'clock I saw them leading off an Armenian whom they had arrested. In the evening my little brother Yohanna, a boy seven years of age, came to see me at the church, saying that my father was asking for me.

Leaving the church I discovered to my surprise that all the Christians I met were in great alarm. I arrived home to find my aunt and other relations weeping, and learned that my uncle Barsom Keshishe, a tradesman, had been arrested. My father, white as a sheet, and very much upset and worried, was speechless in a corner. Not until an hour later did he break silence.

---

[89] "George Kashish" seen in figure 104.

'I was in the market place,' he told us, 'when the Governor came with the Commandant to Government house. There they had a long discussion. A quarter of an hour later the market place was surrounded by the militia, who picked out all Christians over fourteen years of age, arrested them and put them in prison; among them my poor brother Barsom. I managed to save myself with great difficulty, thanks to Kevork Agha, who foreseeing that a general arrest was imminent, advised me to flee. A few minutes later he himself was arrested, savagely knocked about and taken to prison. From a distance I witnessed also the arrest of two brothers, Boghos and Marderos Chatalbashe, Abraham Tasho and many others. I myself was twice arrested in the street, but Providence willed that I should be set at liberty.'

Next day about eight o'clock a public crier announced from the top of the citadel:

'Christians, know that he who does not open his shop as usual will be court-martialed and condemned to death. Why are you afraid? You run no risk. Take courage!'

My father having little confidence in the words of the public crier feared to open his shop. I thought of going myself, but changed my mind, and my uncle, taking the keys, went to open the premises.

Before many hours had passed we learnt that all tradesmen in the market place had been arrested. During the day police agents and soldiers came to our house with a list of names on which figured that of my father whom they intended to apprehend. My mother went to the door and declared that all the men were out. As a matter of fact we had all fled by the roofs to the Bishop's residence, where we found Bishop Mansour in his room, praying. Since our presence might cause his arrest, we left his house, my father taking refuge with Minasse Agha Chatalbashe, and my cousin and I concealing ourselves in the house of Ashour Effendi.

Some time later my mother arrived in tears to say that the soldiers were coming every few minutes to worry her, declaring that at all costs they must have her husband and her sons. They said that they wished to take my father to Government House to ask him a few simple questions, after which he would be released. Fearing that the savages would harm his wife and family, my father bravely decided to return to the house. There he met the soldiers who were waiting to take him. He begged them to allow him to change his clothing and to embrace his children before he left. One of my aunts appeared with her baby in her arms. In her exasperation she said to the soldiers:

"You cowards, you have snatched my husband from his home to take him to Mezre! Now you want to take my brother-in-law! Are you not afraid of the anger of God? What have these innocent people done that you should treat them in this way?"

153

"Do not be anxious!" hypocritically answered the soldiers. "Your men will soon be back home."

Meanwhile the populous Christian quarters were emptied, only a few young people remaining. Almost all the men were taken to Mezre, where they were shut up to the number of fifteen hundred in a large building called "Kirmisi-Konak." No one was allowed to speak to them, but their relatives were permitted to bring them food.

As the Turks said that they only required the Armenians, the Bishop (of the Assyrians), with two prominent members of his congregation, Elia Effendi Tasho and Bedik Zade Arakel, went to see the Governor, the Commandant and the Deputy, and begged them to spare his flock since they were not Armenians and belonged to no political party. Bedik Zade, a very influential Moslem, who was present, asked the Governor with tears in his eyes:

"Why do you treat this unhappy people in this way? They are absolutely guiltless! "

The Governor and his friends then promised to refer the matter to Constantinople, and obtain pardon for the Assyrian community. Some days later a favourable reply did come from the central authorities and thus the Assyrians were spared. In spite of the order, however, the Governor failed to release the fifteen hundred of our co-religionists who had already been apprehended with the Armenians and taken to Mezre. All, without distinction, we outside the town. Happily my father was still in prison at Kharput.

After these events the public crier announced that the Christian inhabitants of each quarter were to quit the town in turn and take the road to Urfa. The Assyrians were to leave on Wednesday. As my father was "Moukhtar" (mayor) he was released from prison to assist in the census of our quarter. On its completion, notwithstanding the order that the Assyrians should be spared, he was reincarcerated.

The public crier repeated the order for the deportations, and the five hundred and fifty-six Armenians and Assyrians prison were released to accompany their families into exile. By good fortune the public crier announced one day that the Assyrians could remain behind. The happiness of our community can be imagined. There were rejoicings everywhere, and our leaders visited the Governor and made him a present of L. T. 500 in gold. At, the same time they begged him to transmit the order of the central authorities for the sparing of the Assyrians the suburbs in which a great many of them lived.

We next went to see the Mudir of one of those suburbs, who had come to town and asked him in view of the order to spare the Assyrian villages. Hoping to gain his favor, we made him presents. He promised to do so, but on returning to his village the barbarian put every one of them to death, even to the women and children. In the little town of Adyaman, hardly a trace of the Christians remained, all of them having been hacked to death with axes and thrown into the river, which watered the locality. The priests in particular had been tortured with indescribable savagery. The following are the names of some of the places inhabited by the Assyrians: the town of Malatiya and the villages of Chiro, Aiwtos and Guarguar.

Three months after the tragedy just recounted, the Governor being absent, all the Assyrians were rearrested one night and sent to the Kirmisi Konak (red prison). A knock came to our door. It was Abdennour, a fellow Christian who wished my father to come to his house. This he did, and on his return he told us that a Turk had been to Abdennour making enquiries for him. It was a tradesman with whom my father had had some dealings, and to whom he owed some money. This the creditor was hastening to claim as he had learnt that all the Assyrians were to be arrested next day. My father's words terrified us and we felt that this time all was over. At dawn my father, my cousin David and I fled and hid at the bottom of a well, requesting our relatives to dig a hole and bury all our valuables and merchandise in a corner of the garden. Every moment we expected the arrival of the wretches who were to lead us to our deaths. At length towards mid-day a relation who was in the secret of our hiding place called down to us from the opening of the well:

"Come out."

"There is nothing to fear. The massacre of the Assyrians has been stopped."

During the massacres of Kharput I lost my uncles, Barsom Keshishe, Boghos and Mardiros; my cousins Nouri and Ohannes, and also Ashour Youssouf, Donabet and Kework Kerbez, who were otherwise related to me.[90]

---

[90] Rev. Joseph Naayem, O.I., Shall this Nation Die (NY: Chaldean Rescue, 1920), 207-215.

Past presidents of the church committee and priests of Saint Mary's Assyrian Apostolic Church, Worcester MA.

Presidents

Dr. A. K. Yousef 1923-4
George Hoyen1925
Nishan Ohan 1926-7, 1934-5, 1941-2-7, 1954
Sahag Perch 1928, 1932
Bishara Perch 1929
Albert Chavoor 1930-6-7-8, 1944
Charles Yoosef 1931
Bishara Chavoor 1933
Gabriel Namen 1943-5, 1950-1
Hanna Namen 1946
Mack Chavoor 1948-9, 1965-6
Dr. George S. Elias 1952-3-5
Afrem Chavoor 1956-7, 1962-3-4
George Ovanes 1958-9, 1969, 1973
Harold Perch 1960-1, 1974
Henry Daughney 1967-8, 1970-1-2

Priests

Favlos Samuel 1927 - 1933
V. R. Peter Barsoum 1933 – 1963
Shamoun Asmar 1963 - 1998

Interviews

Figure 106. June 6, 1934 in Boston, Massachusetts. Sadie Samuel and Youhana Donabed at the entrance to Malcom Donabed's Babylon Spa (convenience) store. The Assyrians of Kharput carried on their Assyrianism into all areas of their lives.

An oral interview with Mrs. Sadie Samuel at her house. Late autumn 1999.

Q: What's your name?
A: My name.(Laughing) You know my name.

Q: No your maiden name.
A: Donabed

Q: Sidoon right. Your first name is Sidoon from the Assyrian word Siyodo (hunter).
A: Sidoon, yes.

Q: Middle name?
A: B. For my father Behnam.

Q: And you were born in Kharput, right?
A: Yes

Q: When were you born?
A: 1911. 10/10/1911.

Q: What did the village look like when you were there?
A: Beautiful. For me beautiful, maybe for somebody else...wouldn't like it.

Q: Was it big?
A: No Harput is a small place.

Q: How far is it from Kharput to Elazig?
A: One hour walking. We only had horse and buggy then. No automobiles.

Q: Where was Kharput, on the top of a mountain?
A: Yes. Such beautiful place, just like a summer resort.

Q: So you had to walk down the mountain to get to Elazig
A: Yes. Elazig is flat.

Q: What did you do during the day?
A: We went to school. I'll tell you a story.
One time my father and mother left my brother Elias and I home. We were only kids you know. They went to Elazig. To a friend's house. Elia said, "Let's you

and I go." So it's snowing like anything, stormy day...kids you know, didn't realize how bad it is. One hour walk in the snow. We looked like Santa Claus. By the time we got there my mother and father were surprised. "Why did you come." "Well why did you leave us alone," I said.

Q: So school during the day.
A: Early morning we went to church. Everyday. Well, Harput is a small place, everything was near each other. Only the market wasn't close.

Q: So what did the village look like? Did it have a lot of trees...?
A: Oh yes.

Q: What kind of animals did you have?
A: Goats, horses, donkeys, dogs, cats, and lots of chickens.

Q: Were their waterfalls and the like...?
A: Ye, in the springtime especially.

Q: Natural water springs?
A: Oh yes.

Q: What did your mother and father do?
A: My dad had a nice trade. He used to dye white cloth.

Q: Did everyone have farms?
A: No. Not many farms. Some, but not many.

Q: Did anyone go hunting?
A: Yes, in the mountains. They caught fish in the stream, hunted deer in the mountains, and there were plenty of snakes. One time Elia and his friends saw a snake in the cave were they used to play. They ran like anything.

Q: Did they...
A: There were no clocks, they told time by the sun.

Q: So did they sing Assyrian songs at weddings?
A: Oh yeah. Lots of them, I don't remember the words.

Q: Were there a lot of miracles and such?
A: Yes we had pilgrims from all over.

Q: What was special in Kharput?

A: When I was a kid going to school they brought a man with chains...my how crazy he was...we had a big stone they tied him there with the chains. He was so bad; he tried to get the kids. He was in there three days and he came out well. The stone in the church.

Q: St. Mary's Church?
A: That's all we had...St George in Elazig was like a house...2 rooms.

Q: What kind of holidays saints, etc. were celebrated by the Assyrians?
A: Saint Mary's Day. St. George.... our church is an antique. Imagine inside, it was cold in the summer and warm in the winter. No fire, air-conditioning, nothing. Upstairs were the *hassios'* rooms. Whoever comes can stay.

Q: Who was more, Armenians or Assyrians?
A: Assyrians of course. Armenians couldn't have many churches either.

Q: How come you had to speak Armenian?
A: The church's fault. Instead of bringing an Assyrian teacher to teach Assyrian, they brought an Armenian to teach Armenian. When matran Abdenur came he said, "Whoever speaks Armenian will be fined so much."

Q: Did you know Assyrians from outside Kharput?
A: Yes. Diyarbekir was not too far, Midyat, Diyarbekir, Mardin. They came a lot.

Q: Did you mix with Eastern Assyrians?
A: There weren't any there.

Q: Did you know about them?
A: Yes, from reading history.

Q: When did you leave Kharput?
A: 1923. My sister, your grandpa (Youhanna), and Benny's father (George) left in 1920. They came with about 100 Assyrians. They didn't let us get to Istanbul for one year.

Q: When you were in Kharput, did they have any Assyrian flags?
A: Of course. On the church. And a beautiful bell too.

Q: Who put the flag on the church?
A: Church committee I suppose.

Q: What did the church say on it?
A: Saint Mary's Assyrian Church.

Q: Was there an Armenian Church in Kharput?
A: Yes, but they weren't allowed to really have it or a school. They went to the Elazig church.

Q: In 1977 when you went back with your sister, were there any people there?
A: Not too many.

Q: How did you feel leaving?
A: Oh. I was very mad. I was crying like anything.

Q: Did you have any Assyrian songs you sang in the house?
A: Oh. Of course. Everything Assyrian.

Q: Did they sing nationalistic songs?
A: Oh yeah. In Istanbul there was more Turkish. I don't know why.

Q: So what does Kharput look like now, after you went back?
A: It's all flat. All the houses are gone.

Q: Were there ancient things there?
A: Yes.... ancient things yes.

Q: Were they Assyrian ruins?
A: Yes.

Q: How did you know you were Assyrian?
A: We just knew; and we had the church. The church told us we were Assyrian. Suryani Kadim, Assori. We are all pure Assyrian. No Armenian in our family.

Q: So we have family in other villages too.
A: Oh yeah. There are many. When somebody died, we didn't have a funeral home. They went to the house and wrapped them in a white sheet and salt. They take them to the church for one night, then the next day they bury them.

Q: In a casket?
A: No, in an old-fashioned thing. Wooden.

Q: When someone died, what did they do? Did they go to each other's houses?
A: Oh. All the neighbors bring food to you. They sing songs. I know the song.

161

It's so sad. Marriot wants me to be happy, but I like listening to the church music. It makes me cry. Special songs when they died.

Q: Did you have problems with the Armenians?
A: Oh yeah. Lots of things. They were so against us. Harput Armenians not others. We have a cemetery in the Elazig church. They tried to bury their bodies there but we didn't let them. That belonged to us. I went to see my uncle and my cousin's grave...Assyrian writing...

Q: Did the Assyrians ever have to go to war?
A: Of course. First, Professor Ashur Yousef. They took him. Poor man. His wife was an Armenian teacher.

Q: Who took him? Why?
A: Turks. The First World War. Educated Assyrians and Armenians. Especially the men they used to take.

Q: What happened to him?
A: They killed him. They killed everybody.

An oral interview with Mr. Kasper and Phyllis Safer in February 2000 at their house in Worcester, Massachusetts.

Figure 107. Kasper Safer at his Massachusetts home. A picture of his uncle, the first Christian police officer in Constantinople, hanging in the background. (2001)

Kasper (Kay) Safer was born in Watertown, MA in 1909 to Aahron Safer and Sophie Atlas. Kay and Phyllis Safer were wed in 1940 at St. Mary's Assyrian Apostolic Church in Worcester, MA. An avid athlete and student of history, Kay frequented places such as New Mexico to dig for gold, and to Kharput to see the birthplace of his ancestors. Kay was known as an excellent speed skater, boxer, and drummer. A naval veteran of WWII, Kay was also a founding member of the United Assyrian Association of Massachusetts. He passed on in the spring of 2003.

Kasper: In Harput there was 1 or 2 Turks there. They were supposed to keep the Kurds from coming in. The Kurds came and massacred every 25 to 30 years. That's how they lived. They used to plunder the Christian villages and take everything. So in later years people used to climb up and go into the church. So what they did was close the opening with stones so you couldn't go back and forth. But the young Assyrian kids used to go up there in the dark as far as they could. The top of the church was flat and could hold like 50 people.

Kasper: I tried to get to Harput as a kid on a boat from Boston but they kicked me off. In later years I have been to Turkey twice and loved every minute of it. And those people are very good to me. In the coffee houses. I told them I was "Suryani Kadim!."

Kasper: Our ancestors destroyed anything pertaining to paganism when they accepted Christianity. We had a lot of different things in the church. The old timers tell me this. They destroyed everything. But lately people have dug there and found different relics of stone. These stones are from Malatyia. We were very strong there. That's 30 miles from Harput.

Q: Is Malatyia the village that all the Assyrians used to live in?
Kasper: No but they were there.

Kasper: On the North East side in a red dirt oval. Tanougli said to me, "Your ancestors are buried there." When the flesh returns to "Adam" red earth or red dust about 150 by 50 feet.

Q: Is it only Assyrians?
Kasper: Yes only Assyrians. It was our cemetery. Later the Turks went and took all the stones from there. I know because my folks used to say that the bishop would come because he could write Assyrian good, so he used to chisel on the stones the names of our ancestors. The only thing that's left is the red oval.

Kasper: Harput is like 3 miles up high. Elazig is down below.

Q: Were there more Assyrians or Armenians there?
Kasper: The Assyrians were naturally there first. We have a church there 179 A.D. I actually have seen a stone in Elazig. The only thing they saved from Harput, with Assyrian writing on it. Bringing it down on a wagon, it split in half. It's still there.

Q: Did they have any legends?
Kasper: I've heard that they put people in chains and in the church, and in the morning they were well. I don't know.

Q: Was there a statue of a horse right?
Kasper: Yes there was. Not too long ago some missionaries took it from Harput. It was outside. That was the only thing the Assyrians left that wasn't Christian. That's why I think we went back to Suryoyo. They didn't want to say we are Othuroyo. But we have proof that Suryoyo is Othuroyo.
The horse.... This Armenian guy Napolean Markarian asked me.... he was from Malatyia...asked me when I got back if I saw the horse outside the church. This was back in his day. It was quite an honor for the Armenians or anybody to come to our church. It was a big affair. They were very religious people.

Q: Do you know when they lost the language?
Kasper: The only thing I can think...the Armenians say they were there first. They weren't there first. They came afterwards. See we were merchants, people working for us digging for ore. On jackasses they used to bring it too Assyria. So you see there was a lot of iron in Anatolia.

Q: Kharput was like a fortress town?
Kasper: Yeah we were a fort.

Q: What did Assyrians do for work, as a trade?
Kasper: My mother's people were Dasho's. They had wealth. They had farms and Armenians working for them. My mother said the farmers used to give half to the Dasho's and half the other half they kept for their people.

Kasper: When I was in Kharput the only thing standing was the church. There was a hole about 2 feet by 2 feet where they would climb to the cliff. They used to get permits from the Turks to build in the area.

Kasper: My father's brother was the first Christian policeman in Constantinople.

Kasper: Our thing was the church. It was everything to us. I know the Euphrates, part of it, used to come down under the church 30 or 40 feet away. That's where they did their washing, and up at the top was the bathhouse on stones. Steam house. There were lots of fights there between the Assyrians and Armenians...that's what I heard. My mother's people were wealthy so they had a stone toilet that went down to the sewer and washed away.

Q: So your mom was a Dasho?
Kasper: Well she was an Atlas. Her father was a horse lover, but got kicked in the testicles by a horse and died 2 days later. Her uncles took her in. They put her to work because she was older. There was 23 in one house. In the fall the farmers would come with their horse team. They had a large room where they would store their harvest.

Q: So what did it look like when you went back?
Kasper: No trees whatsoever. Harput was barren. The soil was rocky. Malatyia was good. They went there to Harput for safety. The Armenians came there afterwards and we protected them. If they were there, they would have the church, not us. We took them in because they were of the same religion. There was also a college there. When I was there I saw one cow. Sheep...but they were happy people with very little.

Kasper: My father was the first Assyrian or Armenian in Watertown. Even in those days, my father was close to the Armenians. From the same area, Turkey. When my father got married he was working in Hood Rubber making forty dollars a week, which in those days most were only making four dollars a week. He became general manager of Hood. In those days if anyone wanted money they came to my father. I have a dagger still downstairs that he gave to people to take to his wife. My mother knew he never parted with the dagger unless for a reason, so she would help those people. But they always paid him back.

166

Q: When did he come to this country?
Kasper: Oh yeah...late 1800's.

Q: So he was one of the first to leave Kharput?
Kasper: Over here there were 5 Assyrians when he came. I know Hope's cemetery on the north side has an Assyrian name. Then they had houses. One man did cooking, and the others worked. They wouldn't go out alone. They went together. But my father. He used to go to the bar room alone. He's got a big record in Boston for banging heads. Dr. Yousef saved his life. They hit him over the head with a bottle. He used to take the lights out first because he was alone, for confusion, then he would break heads.

Q: Did your dad come directly here?
Kasper: He was in Istanbul. They all had to go to Istanbul. He was about 8-10 years old with his father. It took them a month or 2 to walk from Harput to Istanbul. They ate berries on the side and....it was wilderness. With my uncle they were coming and it got dark. So they hid in this hole. They tied a rope on my uncle and him and lowered them down. My father went far until they couldn't breathe. There were stairs going down. There were a lot of historical places like that in Turkey.

Q: So they walked the whole way?
Kasper: I just remember they had to go to Samson...I'm not sure where it is. He came right to Istanbul. An Armenian killed my father's brother, who was the first policeman. Put a sword right through him. So my grandfather was a very religious man who used to feed the beggars on the street. But they killed his son. So he rented a flat on the second floor of this house where the brother and father of this Armenian guy who killed his son lived. So I guess at night he butchered them...like sheep. Then my grandfather himself brought the police. He didn't deny it. He died in jail. But my father said he was the nicest man. But in those days they had a duty to do. They had honor. He wrote a letter to my father before he died, and said he was happy with his life after he got his revenge.

Phyllis: "Assori yemyez, Assori vortim." Assyrian I am and Assyrian I will die. Oh I sound just like my mother. The ladies used to sing it. I also remember them singing about names, chanting, it was their pastime..."Peelav Pilav Donabedis vadi pilav." They are too different words. Peelav is what you eat, but pilav means to go down, break away.

Kasper: East is where the altar is. 20 feet away from the altar there is a stone about 6 feet long and very deep. It's worn away for thousand of years, but still has Assyrian writing on it.

Figure 108. Kasper Safer on his trip to Kharput in the late 1970s. (Castle ruins)

An oral interview with Mr. Harold Perch at his house in February of 2000.

Author: I am going to trace the journey of the people and how they stayed Assyrian and why that was so important to them. How they remained Assyrian over the years. Some came and started the Kharput United Association etc.

Harold: Basically not only stayed Assyrian but also remained Christian. That's how we survived and that's why you find so many Assyrians intermarried with Armenians because similar culture, similar background.... similar religion.

Author: Your dad's side is Perch right. What is your mom's side?
Harold: Barsum.

Author: Oh they're Barsums.
Harold: Now my mother's father over there was very influential, very successful. He had a big business, a good business. He used to deal in textiles and things, fabrics. Imagine in those days he used to go to France to buy his things. In fact my aunt on my mother's side went back to visit Syria and she said, "you know they still talk about my family in the schools there." Now I don't know if that's a fact or not, but that's what she said.

Author: That's amazing that they remember that.
Harold: Yeah. He was a merchant, but he was successful.

Author: That's what Kay was saying. We were talking about why were the Assyrian people in Kharput because it's so far away from the heartland of Assyria, but they always remained Assyrian.
Harold: You gotta remember, Southeast Turkey was a huge center. It wasn't only "Jacobite"-Assyrian, but the "Nestorians", "Chaldeans", everybody was there in Turkey and some went to Iran or Iraq...but basically they're all from near us. Now you talk to Ninos my son-in-law, he's "Nestorian" but he says his mother and father came from today's Turkey. Well they ended up in Lebanon anyway.

Author: Interesting. Obviously in the early period Greek is important to our Christianity?

169

Harold: Well, they're the people that influenced us the most. I was amazed. The thing that woke me up was Saliba, the archbishop when he came. When he mentioned that they were all Greek names and he wanted to keep his own, call himself George. Now that alone should wake them up. Why do we...all the bishops, patriarch....

Author: Yeah Ignatious, Gregorious....

Harold: Yeah it's all Greek. Now I got a lot of stuff on the church. The laying of the cornerstone...it's a beautiful article.

Author: I remember the flag here, my grandmother used to talk about it hanging on the church.

Harold: I remember it used to actually be inside the church at one time. The American on one side and the Assyrian on the other. That was years ago. This is the delegation to the UN, well the League of Nations at that time. Dr. Yousef standing with the Assyrian standard.

Author: I can read her flag. It says "Motho D'Othur," Land of Assyria.

Harold: This is the ascension of the patriarchs from the time of Saint Peter.

Author: I love this.... "The Syrian then in parentheses (Assyrian)." We are basically arguing about a translation.

Harold: That's all it is. Them being over there use Syrian, then these halfwits here are from Syria so they think that's the right word.

Harold: When you think of it these people that came from Kharput were far superior in terms of organizing. They way they built the church. Even their records and things. And they wonder why you get upset.

Author: Does that say John Dasho on the painting on your wall?

Harold: Yeah. He painted that.

Author: Beautiful.

Harold: He died a couple years ago.

Author: What about Captain Dr. A.K. Yousef?

Harold: He was the one that they had a parade for after WWI. My father was

170

with him because he was a veteran too. Marching with a flag and the SONS OF ASSYRIA.

Author: This whole church problem, denying their Assyrian heritage...
Harold: It's a big problem. I mean we've been making inroads for 40 or 50 years and it still seems like we're getting nowhere.

Harold: You know the Albanians in the area offered to help us start a nursing home and stuff. The Orthodox churches getting together. You'd think we'd be involved. We are the only ones not involved. I said to the priest at that time, "Why don't you get with these other Orthodox?"...Since they would never side with the "Nestorian" or "Chaldean" Assyrians, He said, "They're different kinds." So I said... "Explain to me how they are different." He wouldn't answer me.

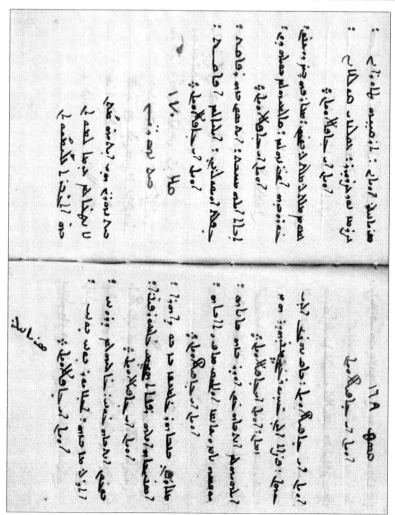

Figure 109. *Malphono* Naum Faik's "Beth Nahrain" poem as was sung in Kharput and in America by Kharput and Diarbekir Assyrians alike. This copy stems from the pages of one of Youhanna Donabed's books of national and church songs. Much of it composed in (serto) Assyrian but Ottoman Turkish in language.

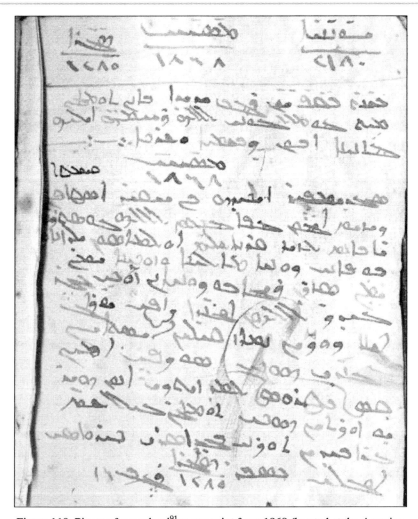

Figure 110. Pieces of a garshuni[91] manuscript from 1868 (located at the Assyrian Manuscript Foundation, coll. Farajallah Hanun Fathi) Notice the years at the top. *Hajiyo* (Muslim), *Msiḥoyo* (Christian), *Younoyo* (Greek).

---

[91] A term usually used for Arabic written in the Syriac script, or vice versa. Thus this type of "garshuni" may as well be Turkish garshuni.

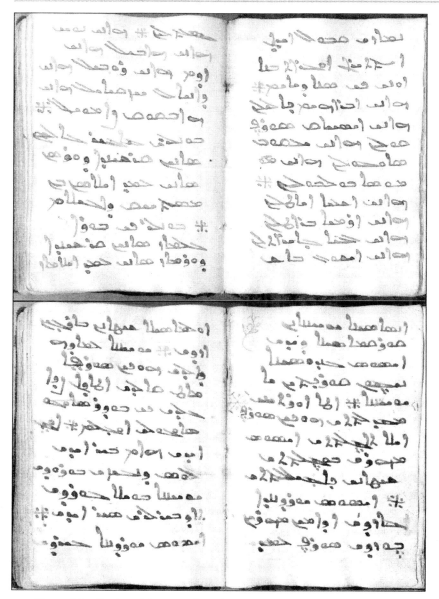

Figure 111. Continued from previous figure (located at the Assyrian Manuscript
Foundation, coll. Farajallah Hanun Fathi)

Index